AF326832

Layers
of
Light

Photographs by
Dag Alveng 1979-1994

Words by
Michael Almereyda
Per Hovdenakk
Susan Kismaric
Per Charles Molkom
Gertrud Sandqvist
Atle Skageng
Andrzej Zych

Published by
Ex Libris Publishers AS

This book is being published in connection with
the exhibition "Layers of Light" at the Henie-Onstad Kunstsenter,
Høvikodden, Norway
November 19 1994 to February 5 1995

Copyright© 1995 Dag Alveng
Editor: Carole Kismaric
Project Manager: Atle Skageng
Design: Per Charles Molkom
Translation: Michael Garner
Henie-Onstad Kunstsenter
Andrzej Zych
Halftone Photography in Quadratone
by Thomas Palmer
Printing Consultant:
Richard Benson
Typesetting: Bates Advertising, Per Schenk
Printing: A.s Merkur-trykk
Paper: 170 g Phoenomatt by Scheufelen,
delivered by Basberg Papir AS
Production supervised by
Grafisk Service Knut Grønli AS, Oslo, and Dag Alveng

This book is supported by
The Norwegian Council of Cultural Affairs
and Norsk Fotografisk Fond

Printed and bound in Norway

ISBN 82-7384-471-4
Published by Ex Libris Publishers AS
The English edition of "Layers of Light" is distributed
by D.A.P./Distributed Art Publishers, 636 Broadway,
New York City, New York 10012
Tel: 212 473 5119 Fax: 212 673 2887

Layers

New York 1986-1994
Summer Light 1979-1994
France 1980
Works 1980-1987
Asylum 1979-1982

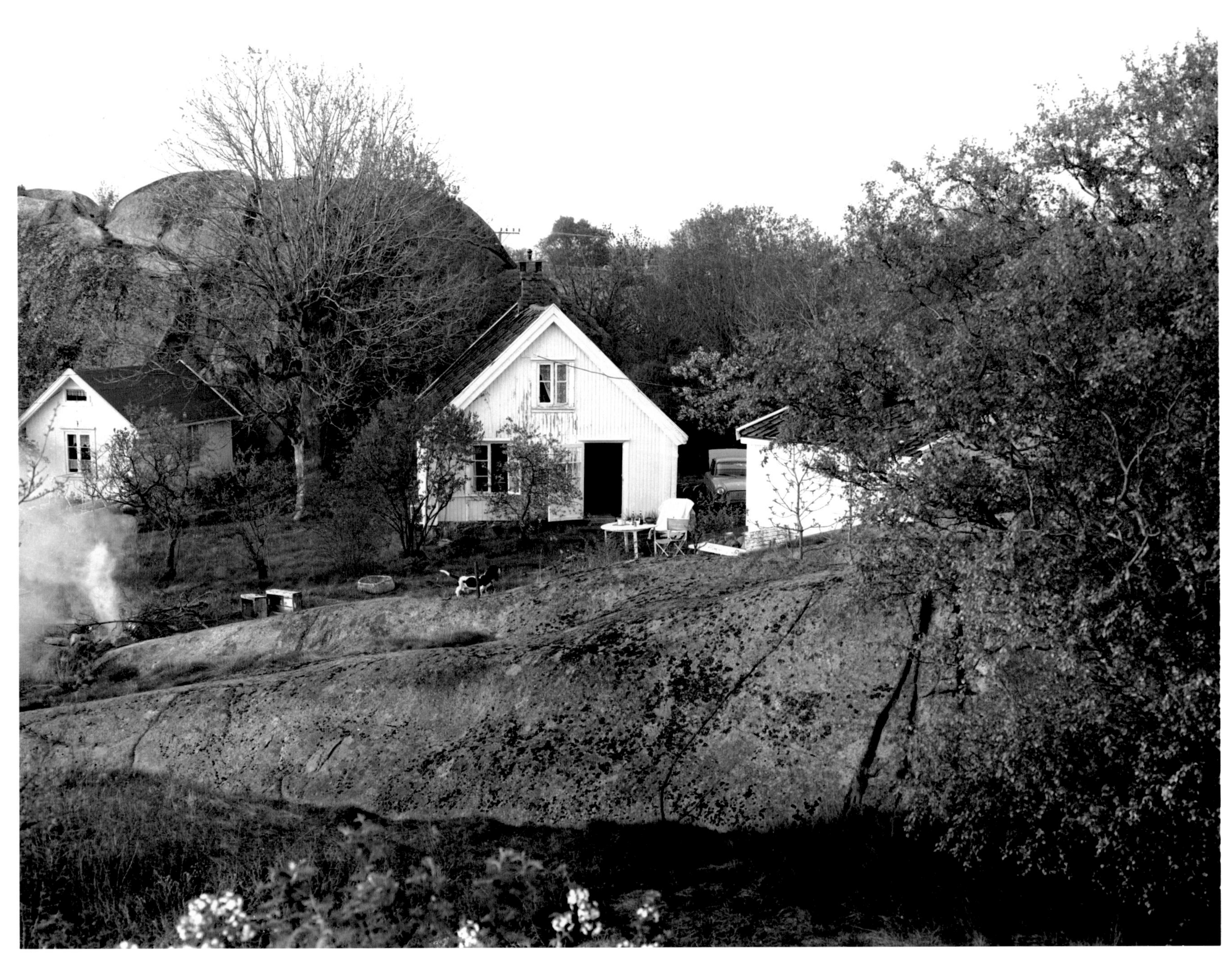

Maureen's Place, Hvasser. 1981

Foreword

The photographic community in the Nordic countries is a small one, and it has limited resources. While receptive to outside impulses, few Nordic photographers can point to an independent reworking of ideas that inform the history of photography.

Dag Alveng is a rare exception among Nordic photographers. He has attached great importance to participating in the photographic community outside Scandinavia. By exposing himself to influences from a broader context, he has been able to pursue his own ideas with great determination, and has strived to achieve a higher level of perfection than is usual in the narrower Norwegian context.

Active for nearly twenty years, Alveng's output is extensive. Very early on he settled on a core of ideas, which he has subsequently developed in individual pictures and in his series. It is therefore natural for us now to view Alveng's pictures in a retrospective context—to survey the development of his oeuvre and his systematic working out of his central themes.

Per Hovdenakk

Eyes That See

Some people see things more clearly than others. Indeed, they see with such intensity that it is difficult for them to live with the loss that arises when what impresses them vanishes.

Throughout history, such people have developed a special gift: the ability to recreate, relate, and interpret certain fleeting phenomena which arise, only to disappear again. These people have a pressing need to capture and mold each impression so their fellow men can rejoice in, or perhaps, reject something they cannot experience themselves.

One of those who is blessed with this special gift is Dag Alveng. Using photography as his medium, he shares the wealth of his impressions willingly with the rest of us–those of us who pass an open gate without attaching any importance to it, apart from the fact that somebody has forgotten to shut it. Those of us who look upon the dazzling summer light as an irritating quirk of nature, to be kept under control by our Ray Bans. Those of us, too, who wander through the city, but have to take aspirin at the end of the day because of all the people and cars.

There are two kinds of eyes: eyes that see and eyes that skim. Let's suppress the need to skim the pictures in this book. Let us see what Alveng has seen.

Per Charles Molkom

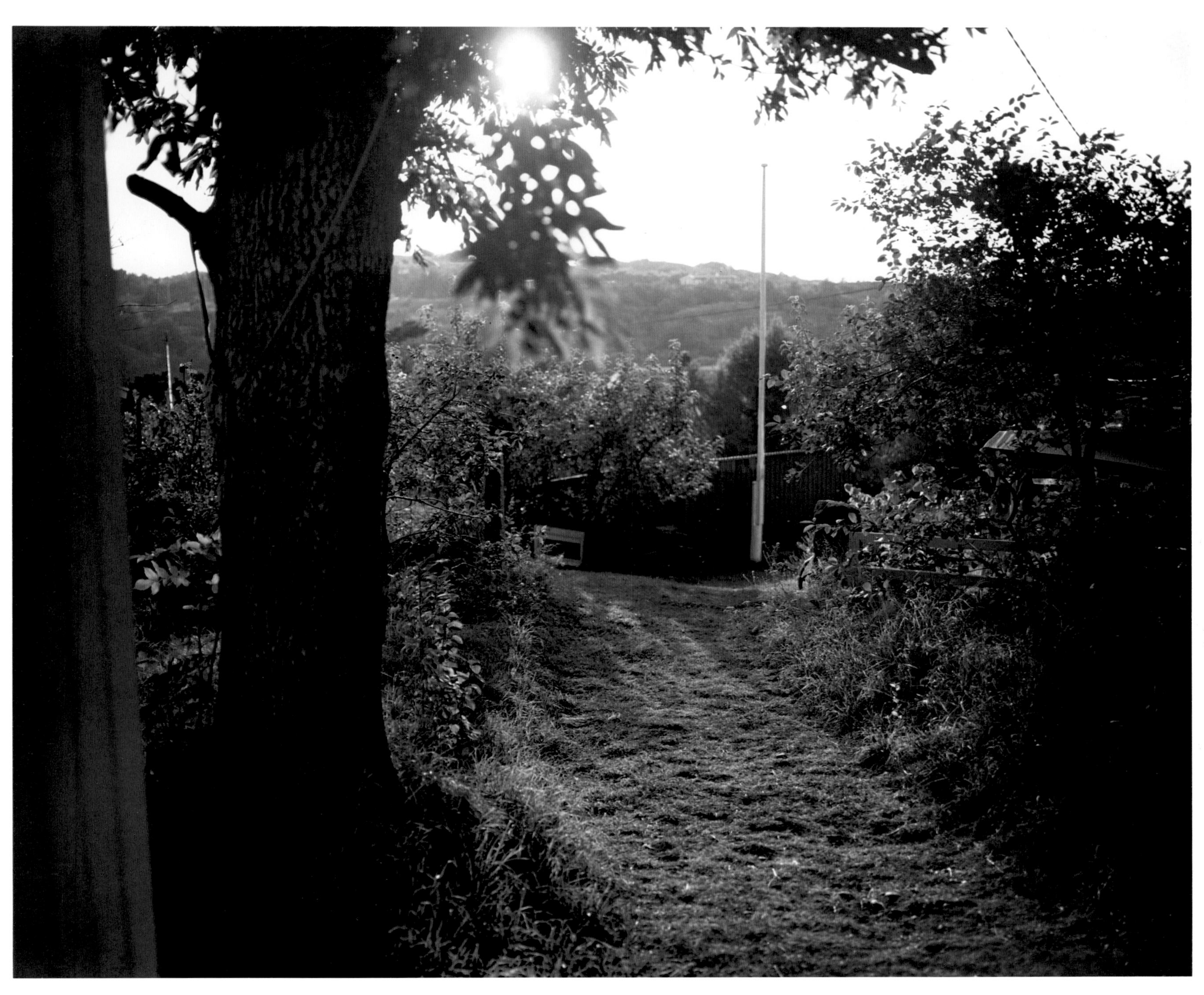

Sunset, Hvasser. 1981

New York

1986-1994

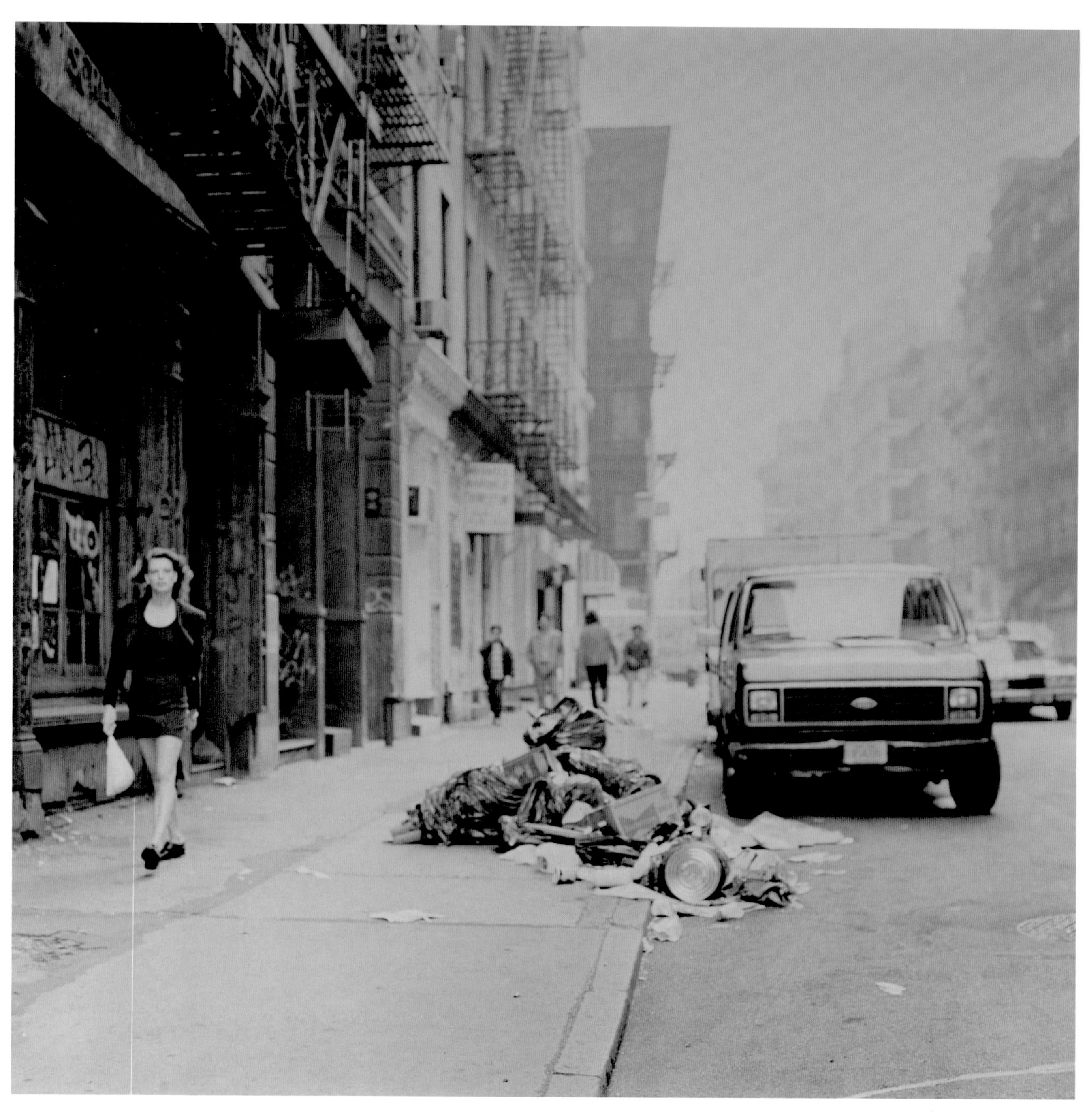

Woman and Van. 1989

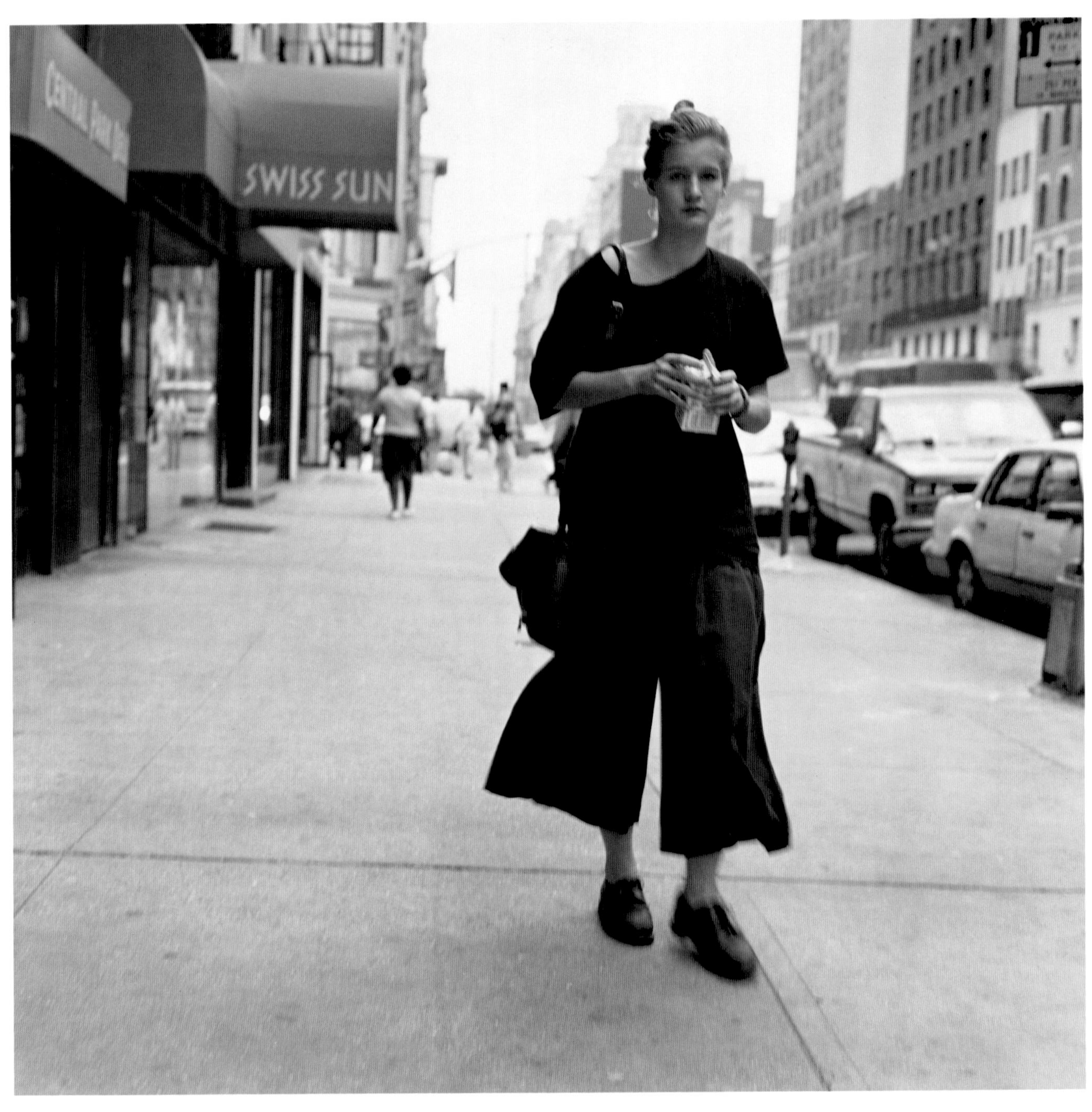

Swiss Sun. 1990

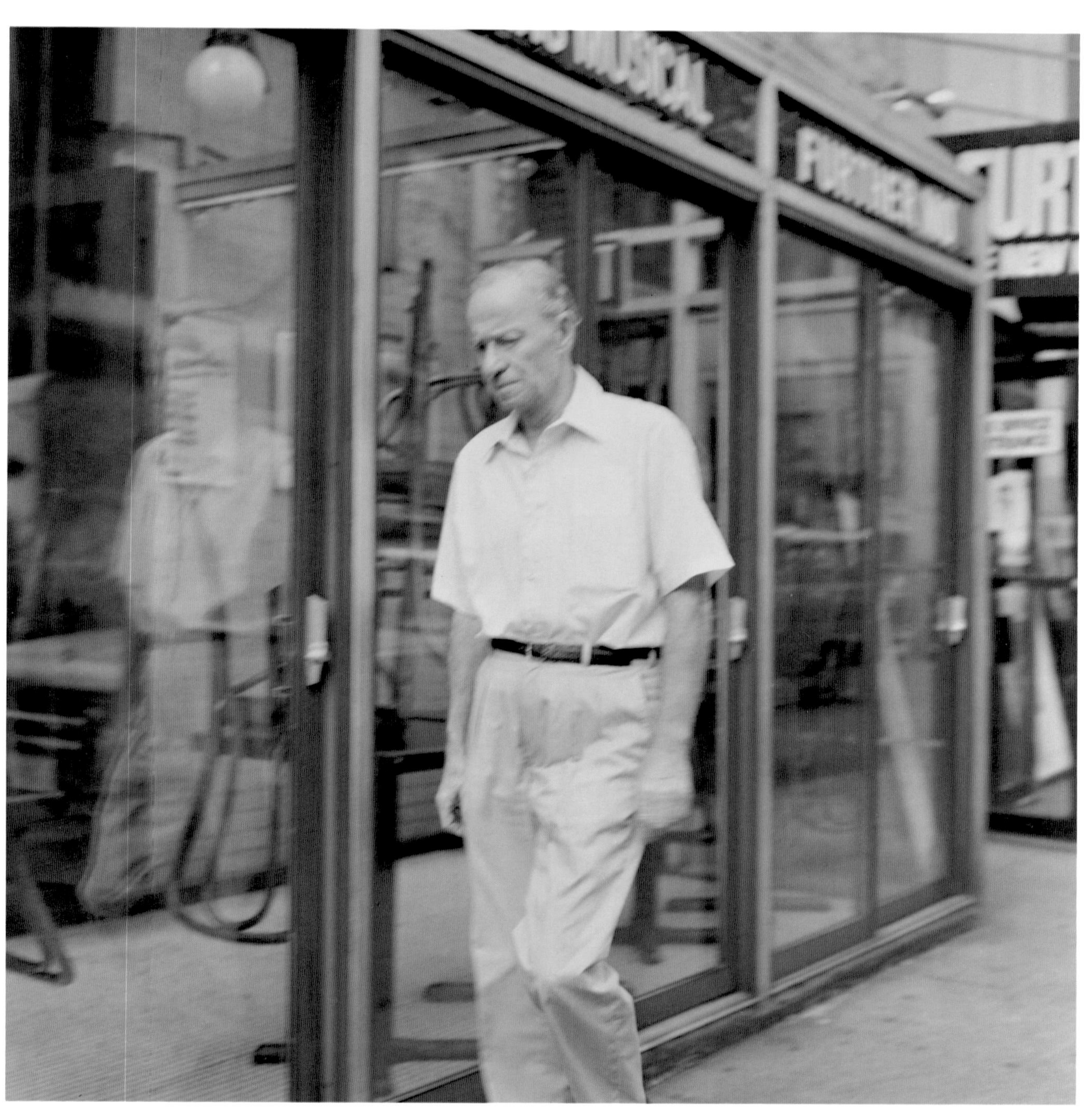

Man Looking Down. 1990

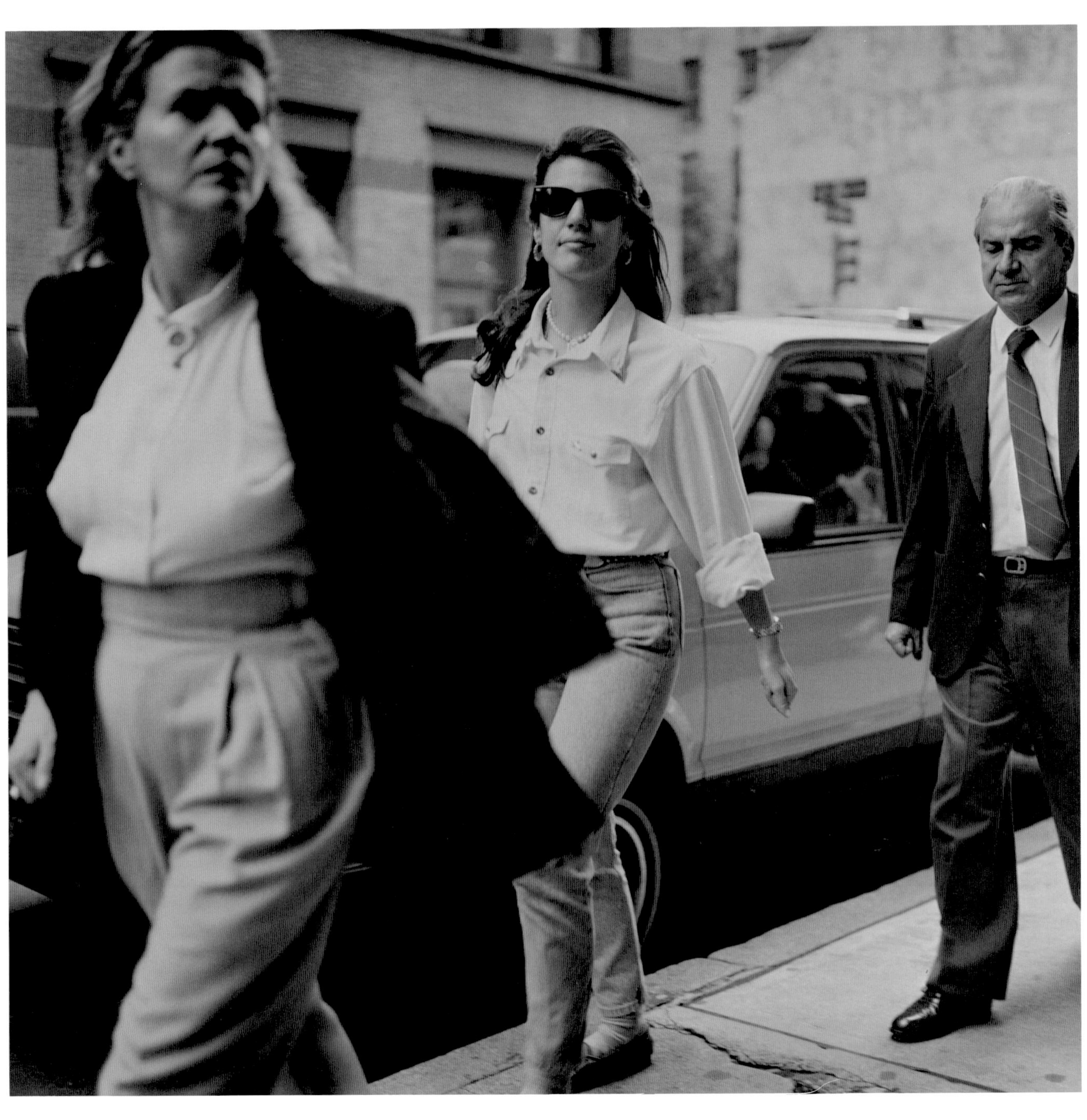

Woman with Open Jacket. 1989

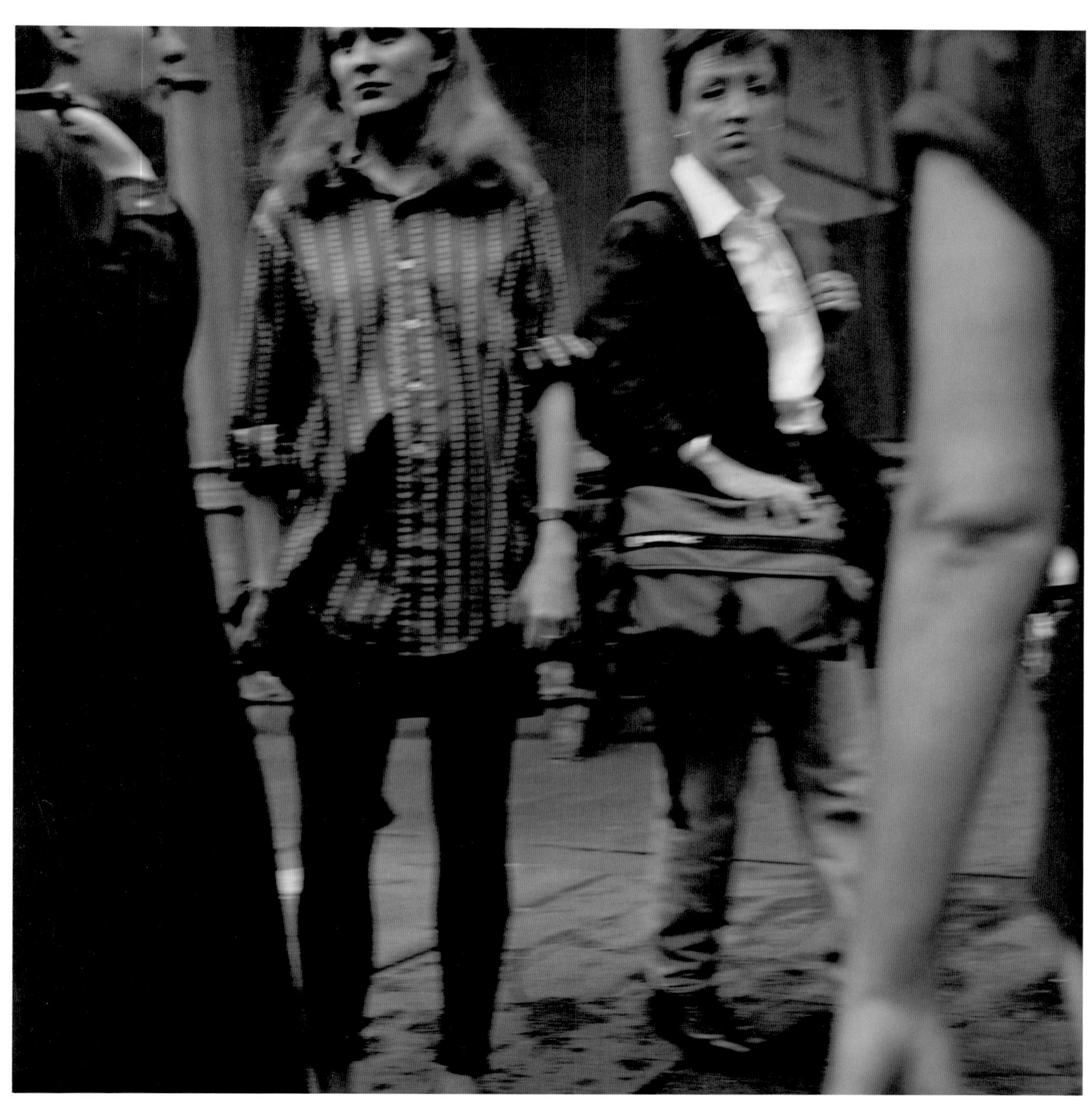

Dark Picture, Four People. 1990

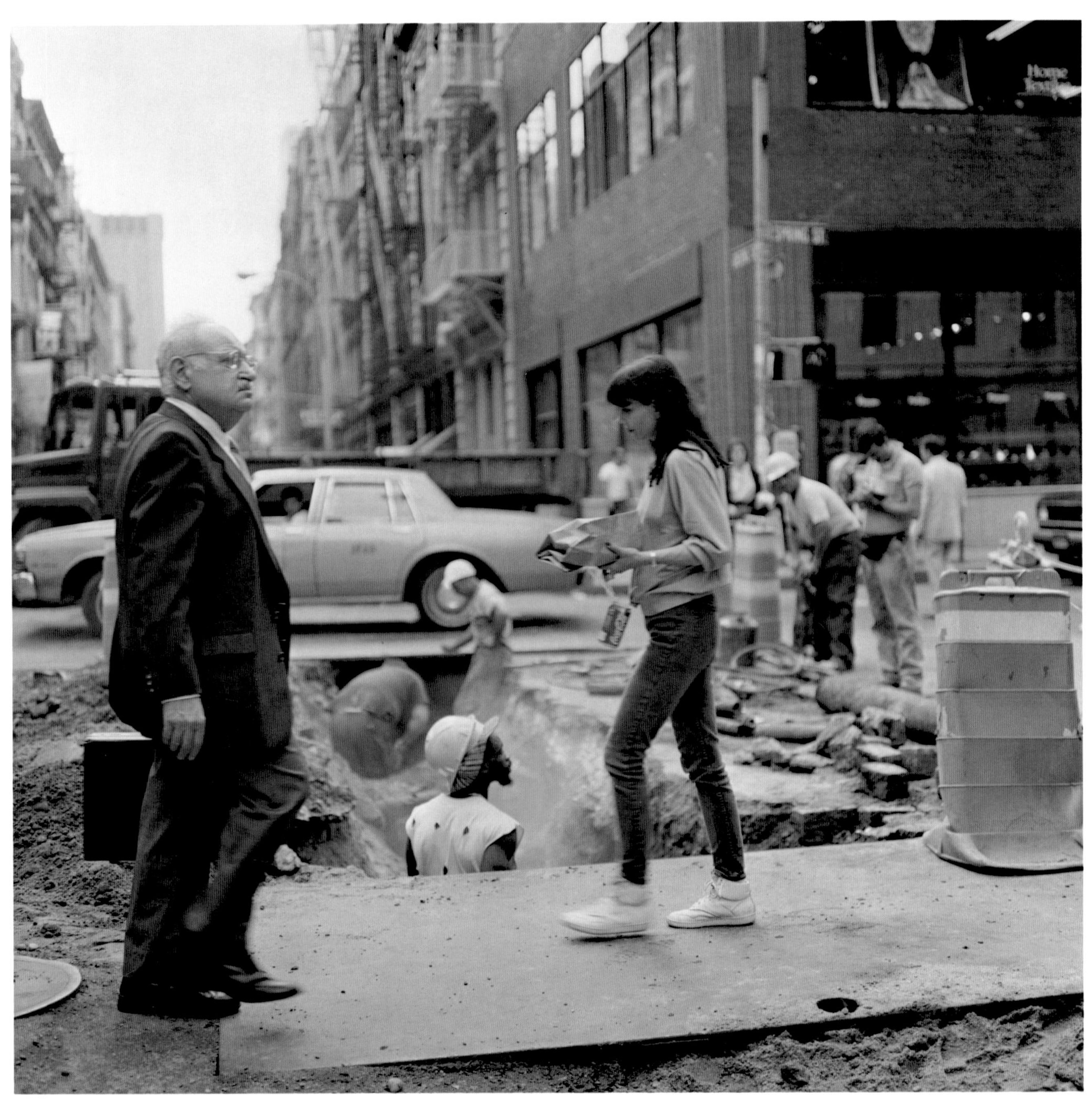

Construction. 1990

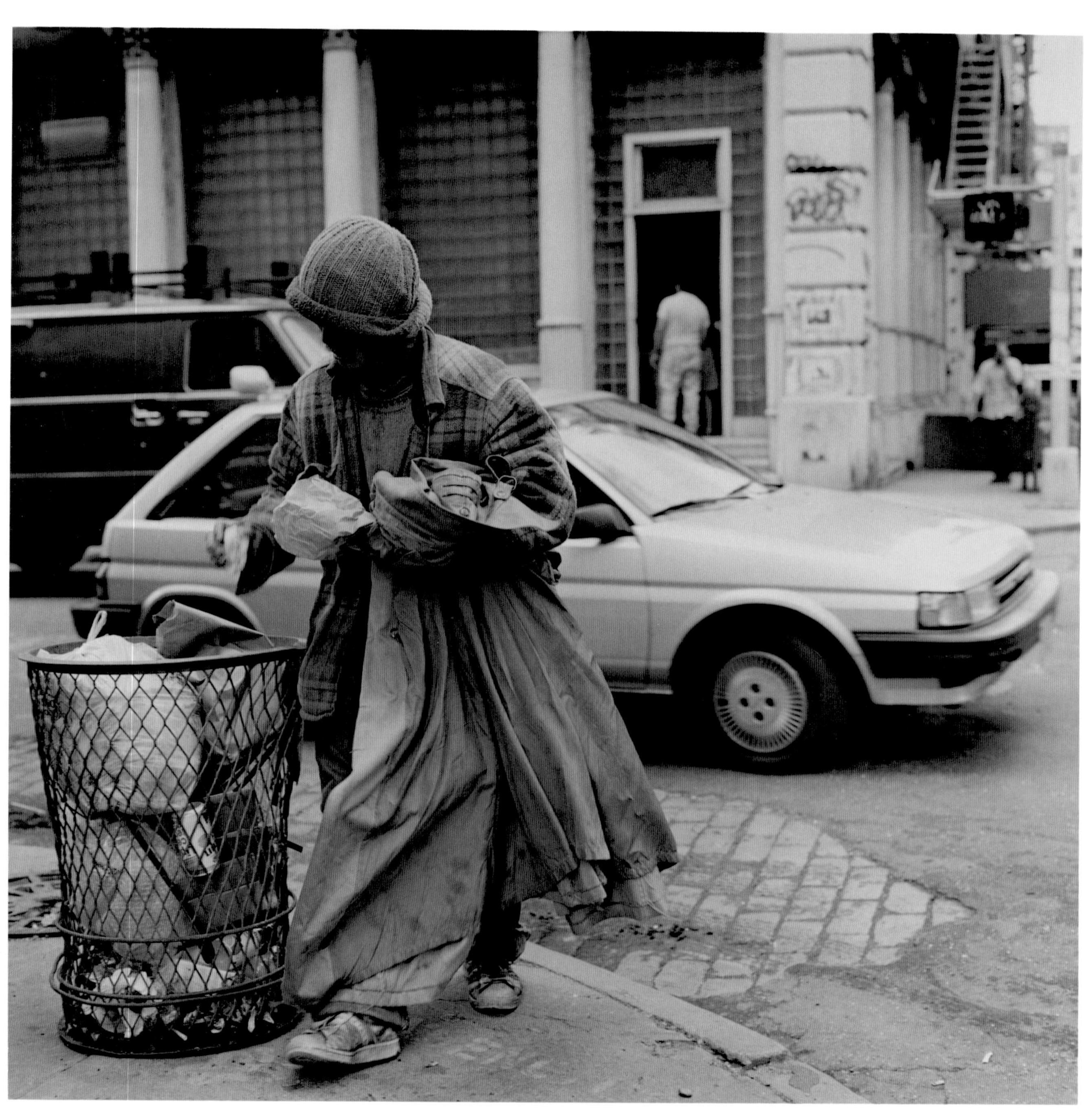

Man Looking in Garbage Can, Coat in Hand. 1990

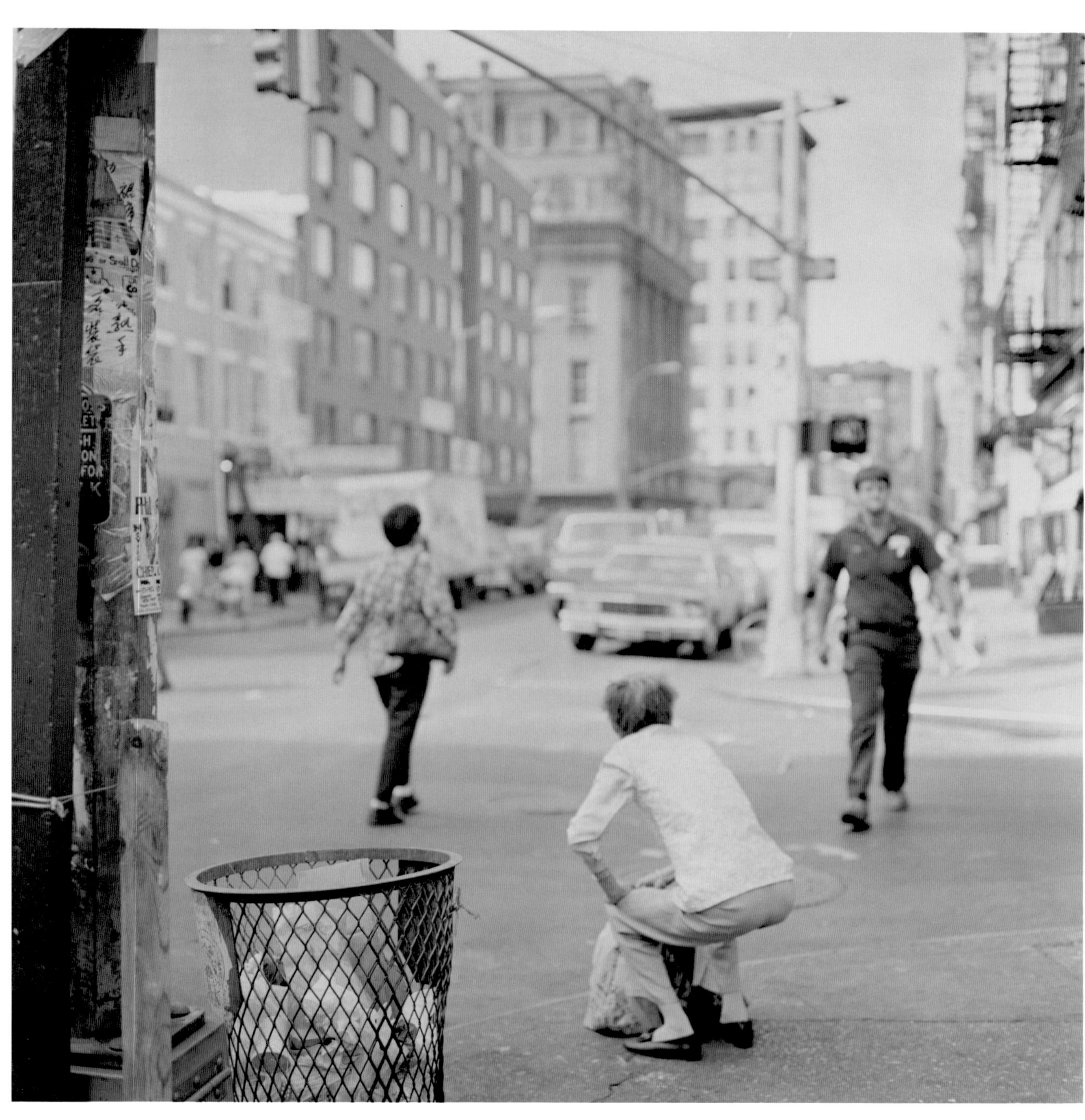

Chinese Man Bending Down. 1990

The Man of the Crowd

These photographs could be safely regarded as formal experiments, pictorial conjuring tricks, a record of the random miracles of New York sunlight. But to review these images so narrowly would lead away from what is most compelling and strange in them—a certain aloofness and anxiety operating within the ecstatic display of technique.

Alveng is clearly uninterested in familiar street drama. He stays away from narrative incident of all kinds, avoids confrontation, direct eye contact, and sweeps the stage clear of the routinely vivid street theater repertory company—gangster-like businessmen, alluring women, the homeless. Instead, Alveng's camera presents a city of shadows and sleep-walkers, a place populated strictly by strangers. The fractured, doubled imagery mirrors Manhattan's overlay of rich and poor, people hurrying to the next thing amidst those just barely getting by. You can feel, within these juxtapositions, Alveng's detached but tender, even baffled, regard for his fellow creatures. The people in these pictures are nearly all alone, looking lost or adrift, their faces, when visible, locked in soft blank stares. A procession of ghosts engaged in haunting themselves.

Taking the pictures as a series, I think less of other photographs than of certain stories by Edgar Allan Poe. Alveng's cluttered yet controlled double exposures radiate a Poe-like quality of fine tuned dementia. You sense that for all their formal dexterity and wit (the high heels prancing from the man's shadowy trousers on page 36; the woman caught in the web of a trash can's meshed lines, page 27) there is something else going on, and the spectacle of eclipsed or colliding realities registers as a muffled declaration of anguish, panic, loneliness.

I think particularly of a neglected Poe story called "The Man of the Crowd," in which one of the author's typically raw-nerved narrators, recovering from a long illness, follows an old man through a crowded London street.

This old man, the narrator has determined on first seeing him, is the "incarnation of the fiend." A criminal whose despairing face reflects a wild history. Pushing through the crowd, increasingly astonished and exhausted, the narrator tracks the man through fog and rain, in and out of shops, down twisting streets and alleys. The old man has no apparent destination, talks to no one, keeps doubling back on himself, staggering, an air of urgency alternating with a look of vacillation and unease. But he doesn't stop, and never once glances back at his pursuer.

Finally, in one nightmarish paragraph, in a telescoping of time not unlike a series of double exposed photos, daylight chases away the night, and as quickly night falls again, and the old man picks up speed as if invigorated by his aimlessness and despair—until the narrator finally and desparately overtakes him, looking him full in the face. But the old man doesn't see him, keeps on walking. The narrator, "wearied unto death," lets him go: "This old man," I said at length, "is the type and the genius of deep crime.

He refuses to be alone. He is the man of the crowd. It will be in vain to follow; for I shall learn no more of him, nor of his deeds."

Poe was serving up a description of the demonic, devouring aspect of city life, the tidal energy and implicit violence flowing through any modern, urban crowd. And as in Alveng's photos, you sense a metaphor at work, a metaphor for an artist's relation to the world, a search in which it's possible to match the narrator/photographer with his targeted subject, taking their measure as interdependent doubles, at once detached and engaged, commited and lost, and mutually, inescapably guilty of the city dweller's simplest buried crime: fear, particularly fear of solitude, a deep unbreakable loneliness.

Dag Alveng, walking the streets of a foreign city, has come up with a group portrait of phantoms dissolving into space like fogbound ships. I can imagine similar pictures flashing before the eyes of Poe's deeply disconnected narrator or even, for that matter, before the eyes of Poe himself when, four years after he composed this story, he was found crumpled in the gutter of a downtown Baltimore street, delirious, wearing another man's clothes. He died four days later, forty years old. Listed cause: "Congestion of the brain."

Michael Almereyda

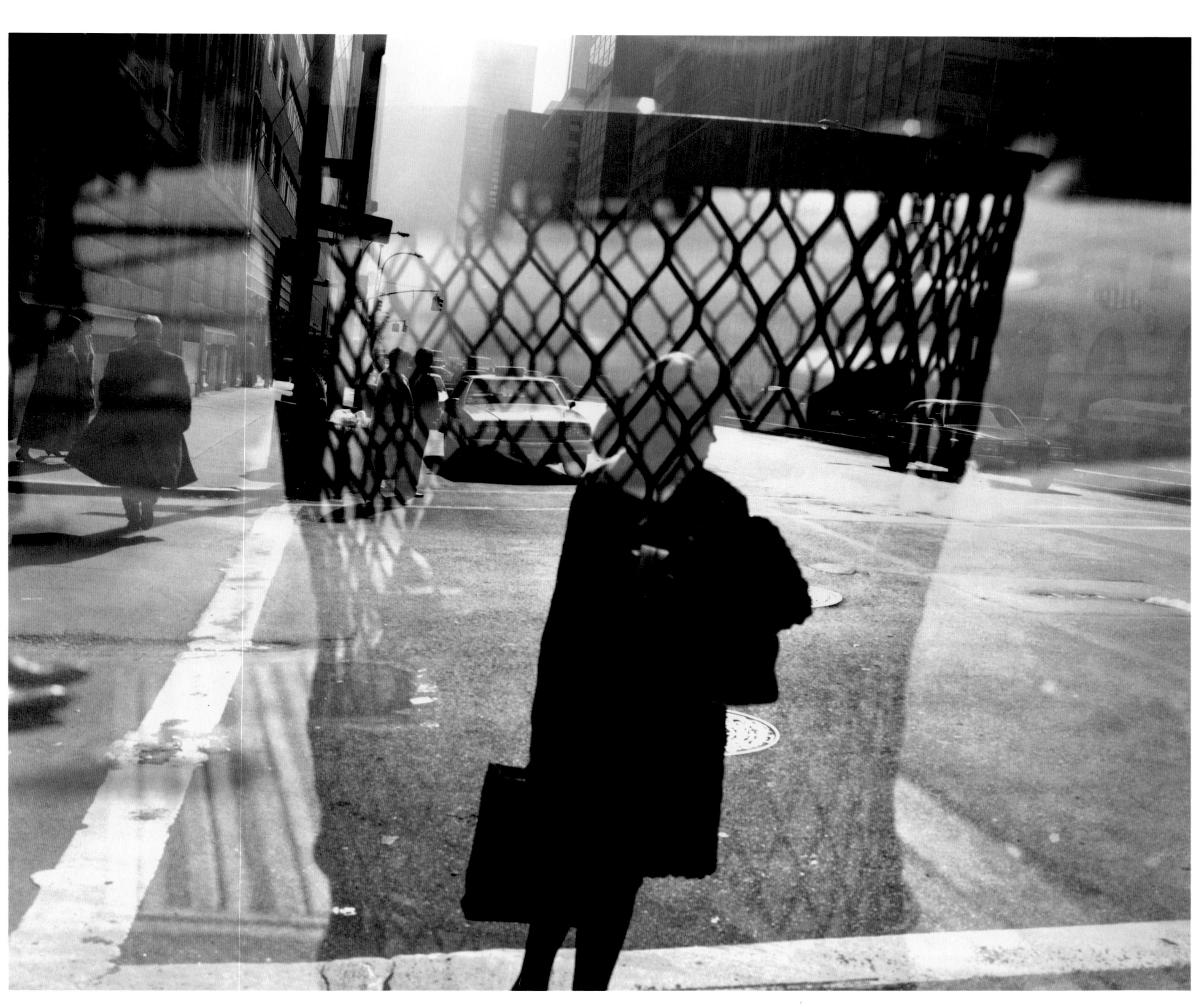

Woman in Garbage Can. 1991

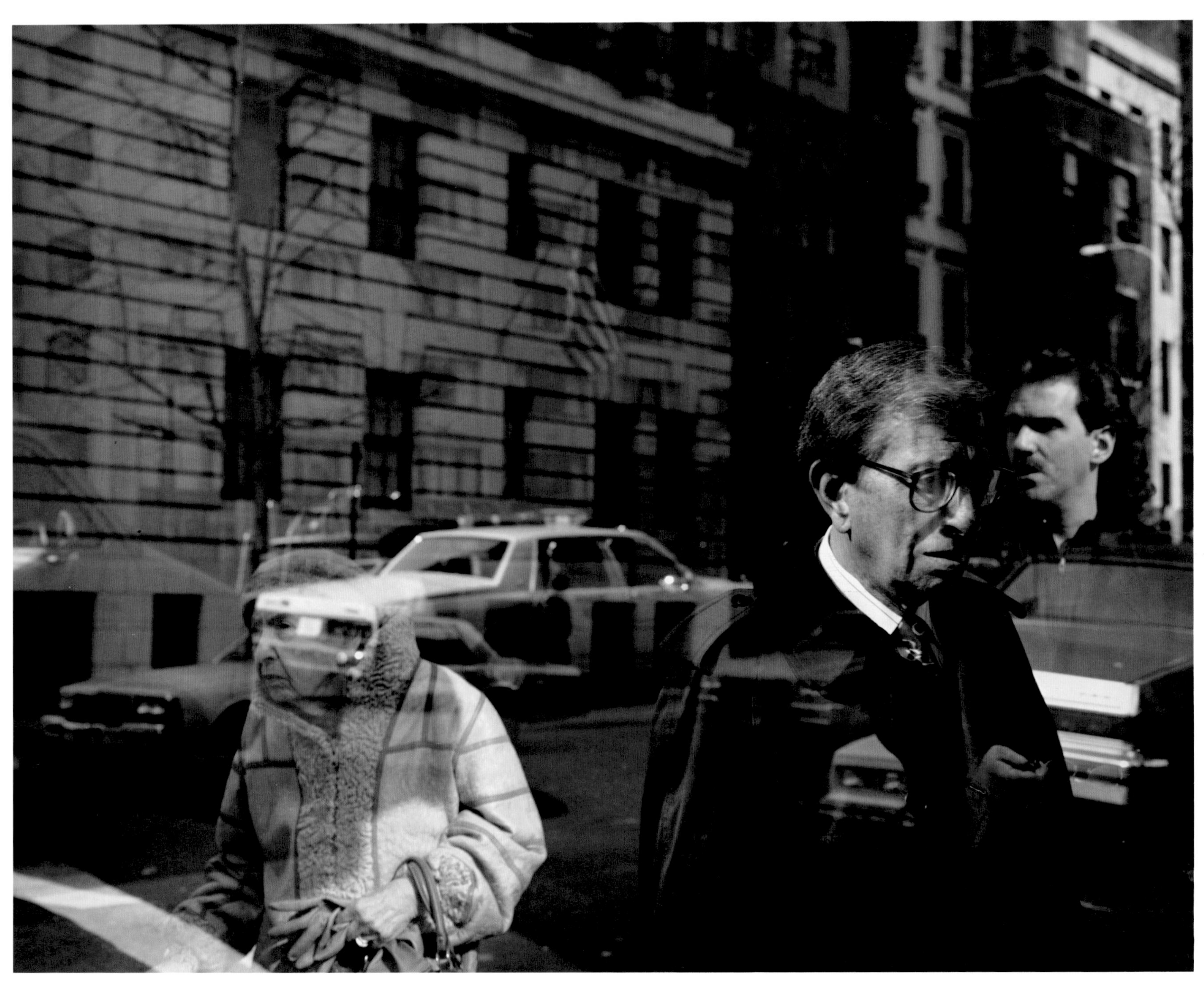

Three Faces. 1991

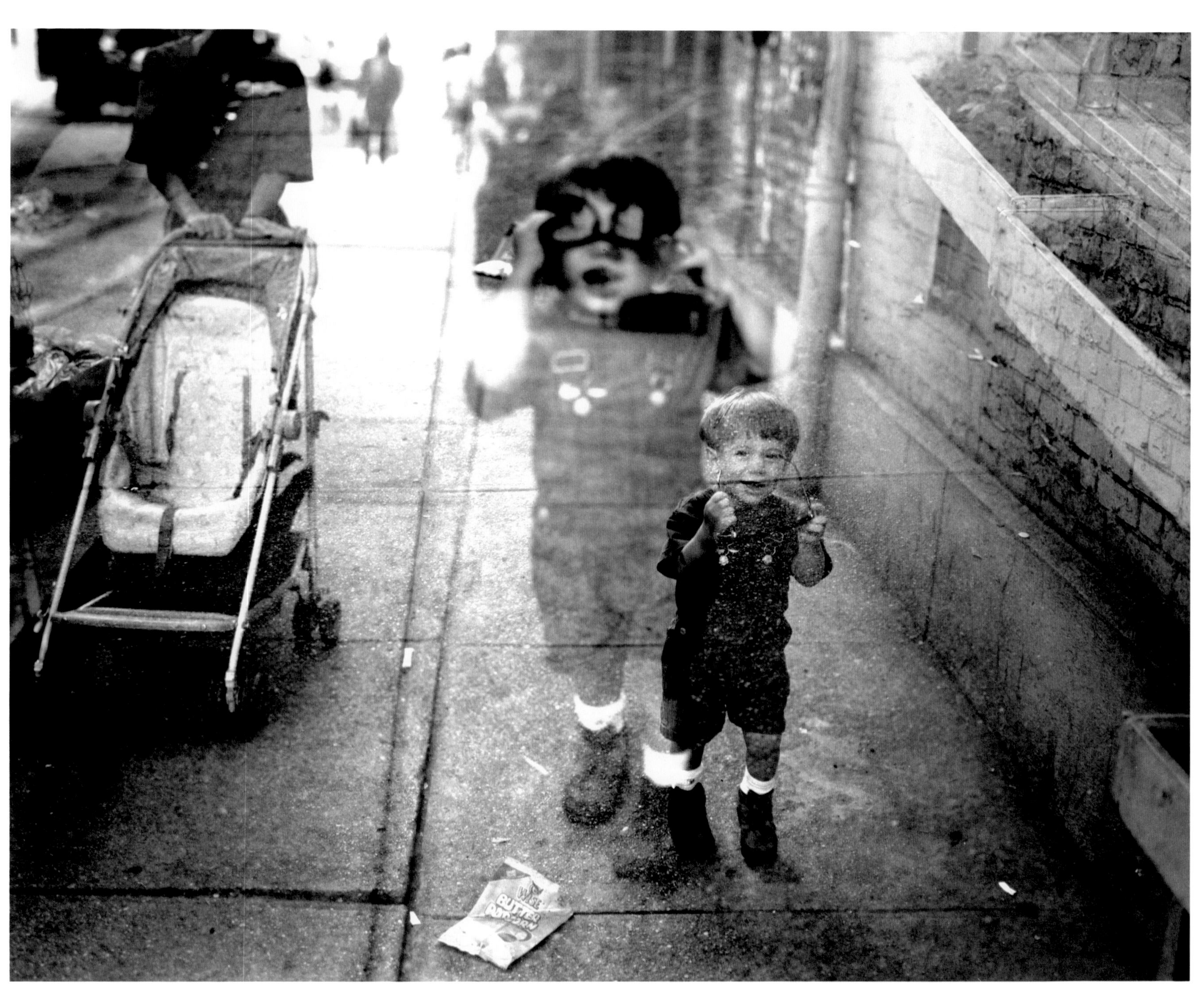

Boy with Glasses. 1994

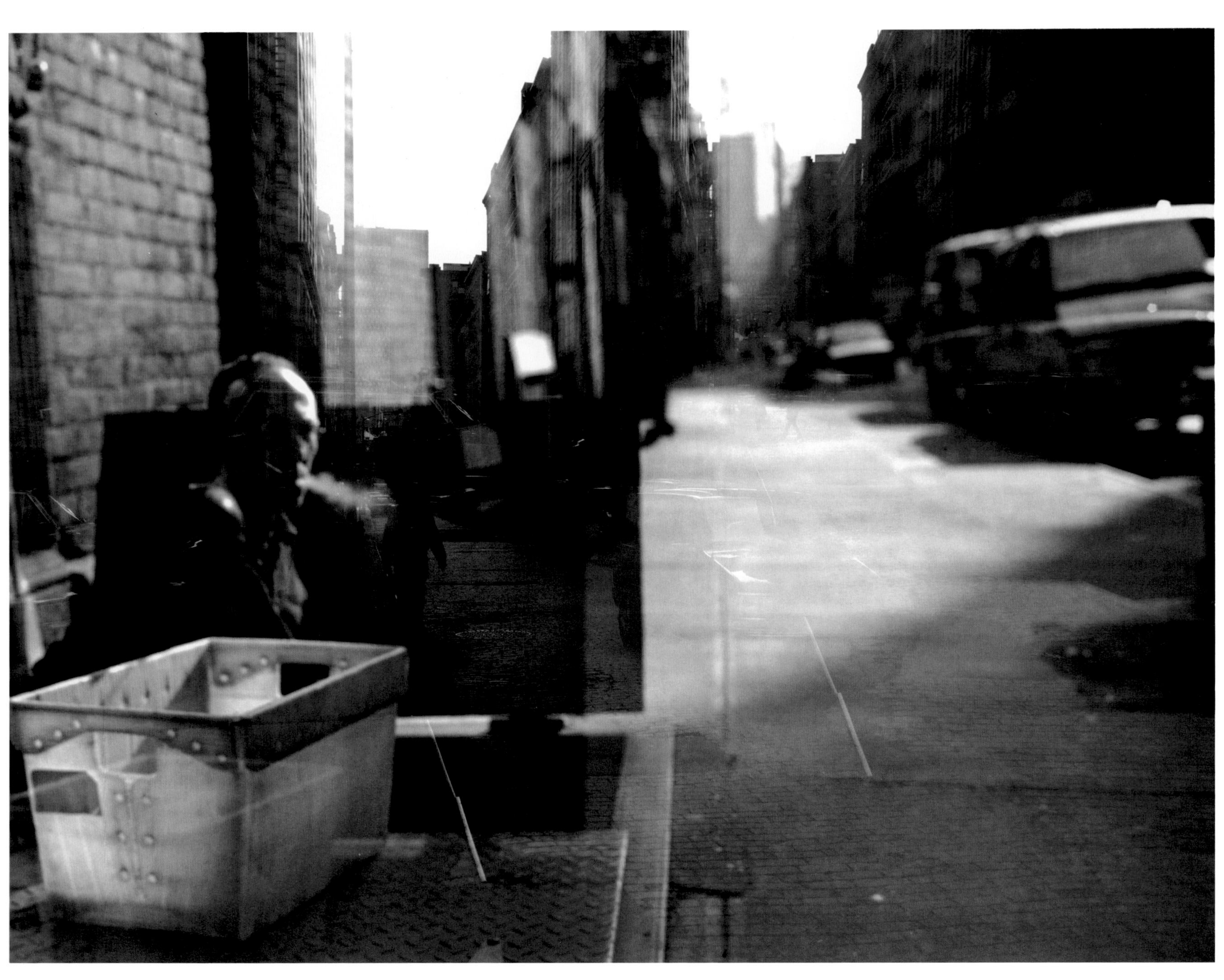

Man and Cigarette Smoke. 1991

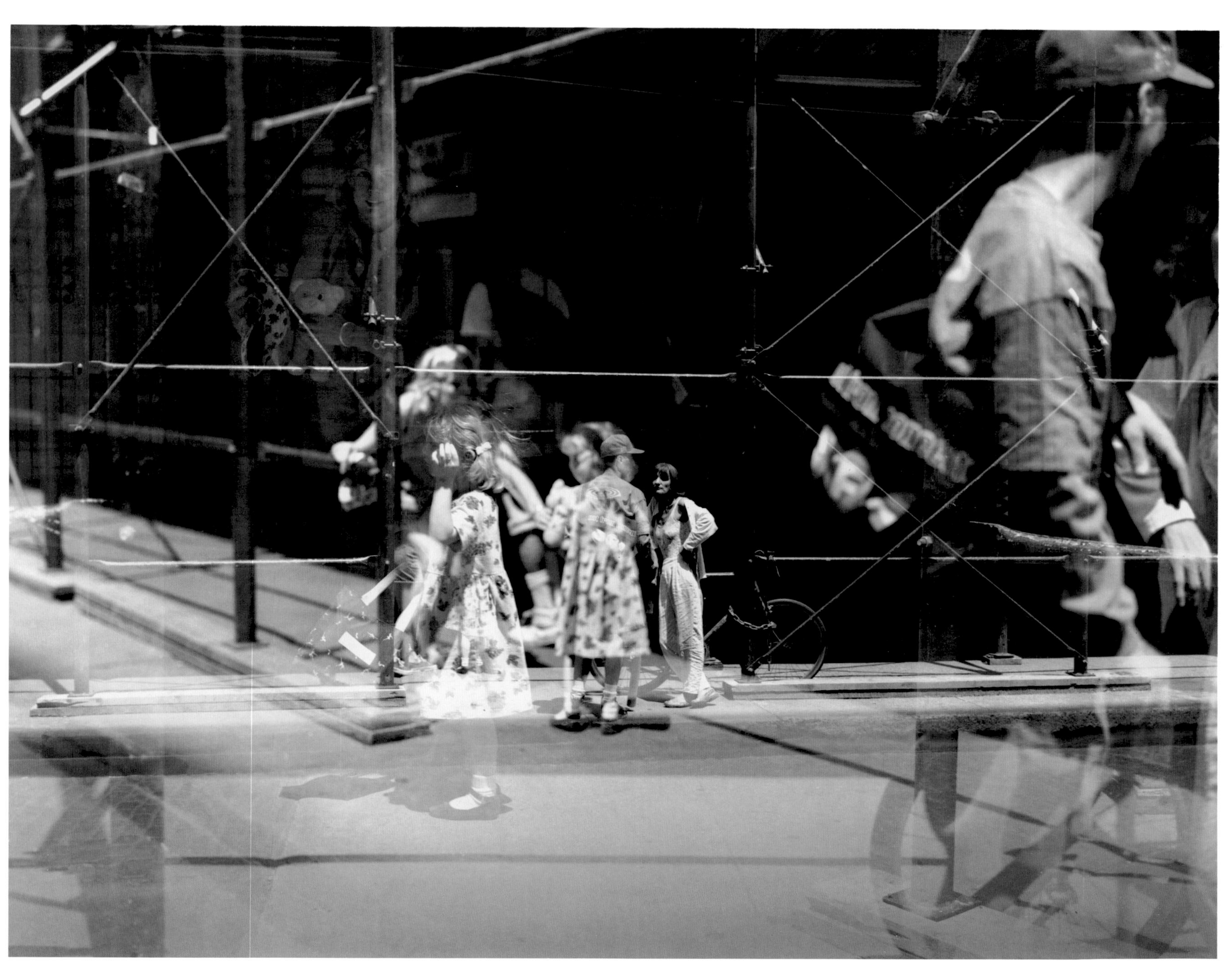

Girl with Dress. 1993

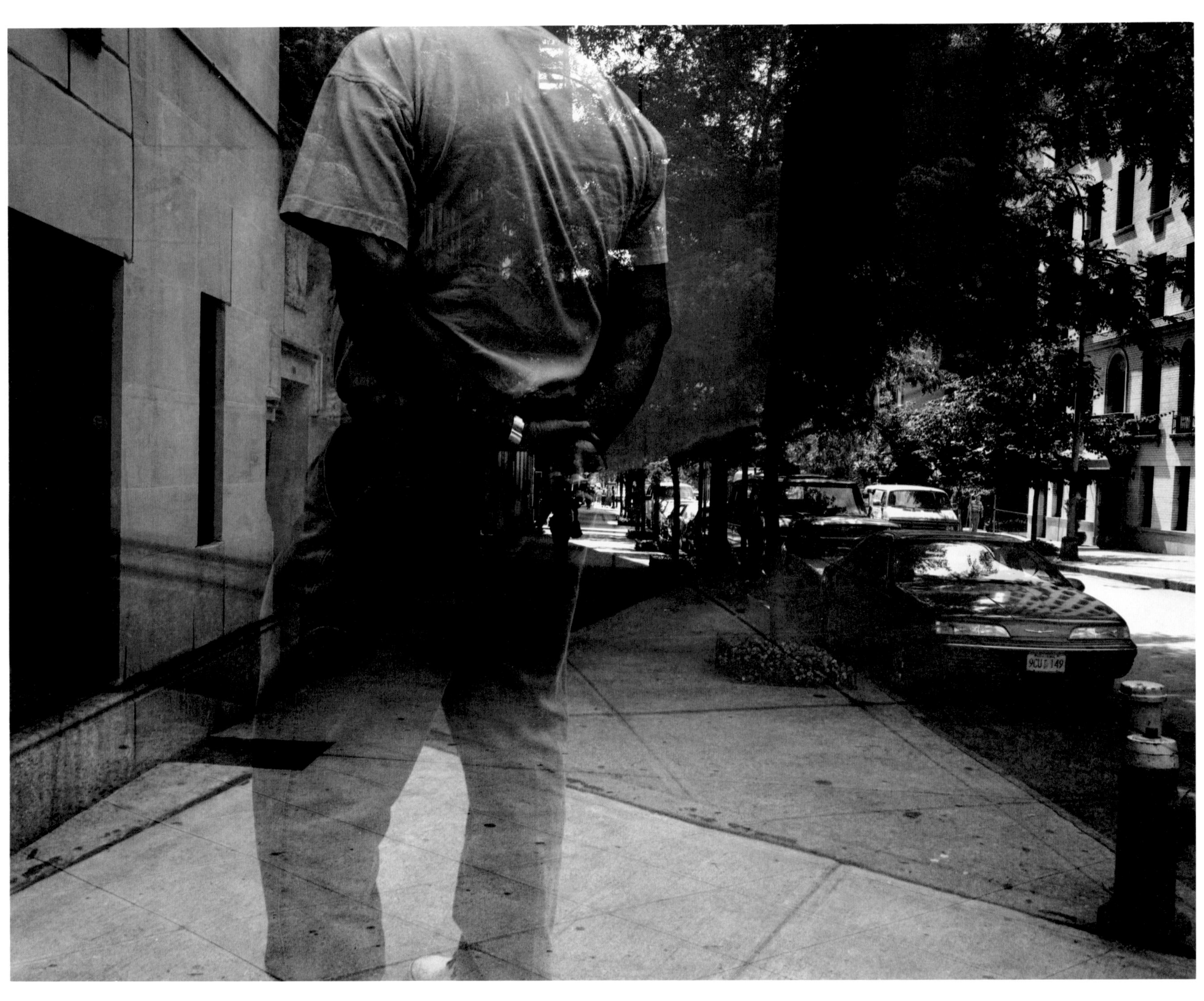

Man with Back to the Camera. 1992

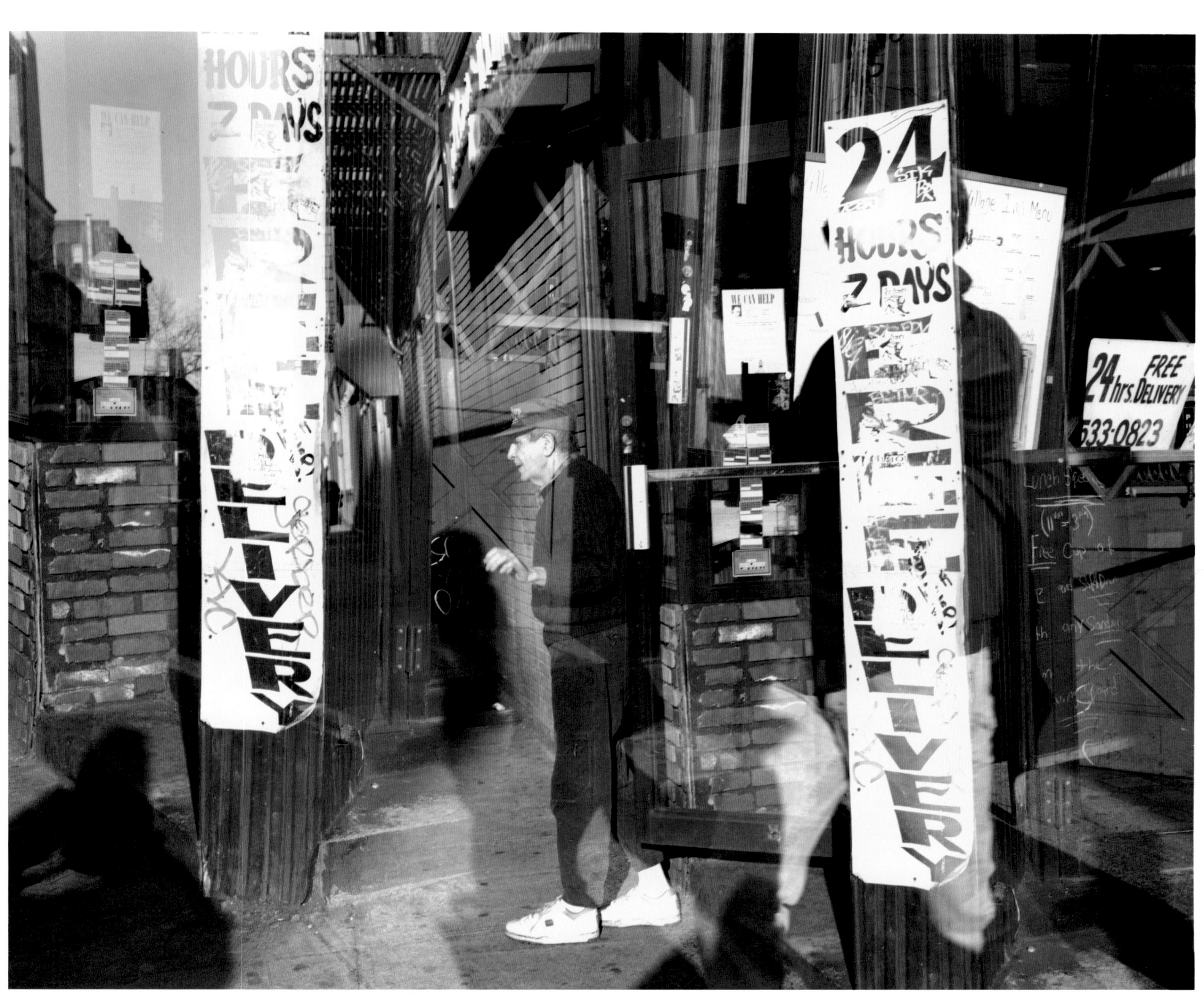

24 Hours Free Delivery. 1993

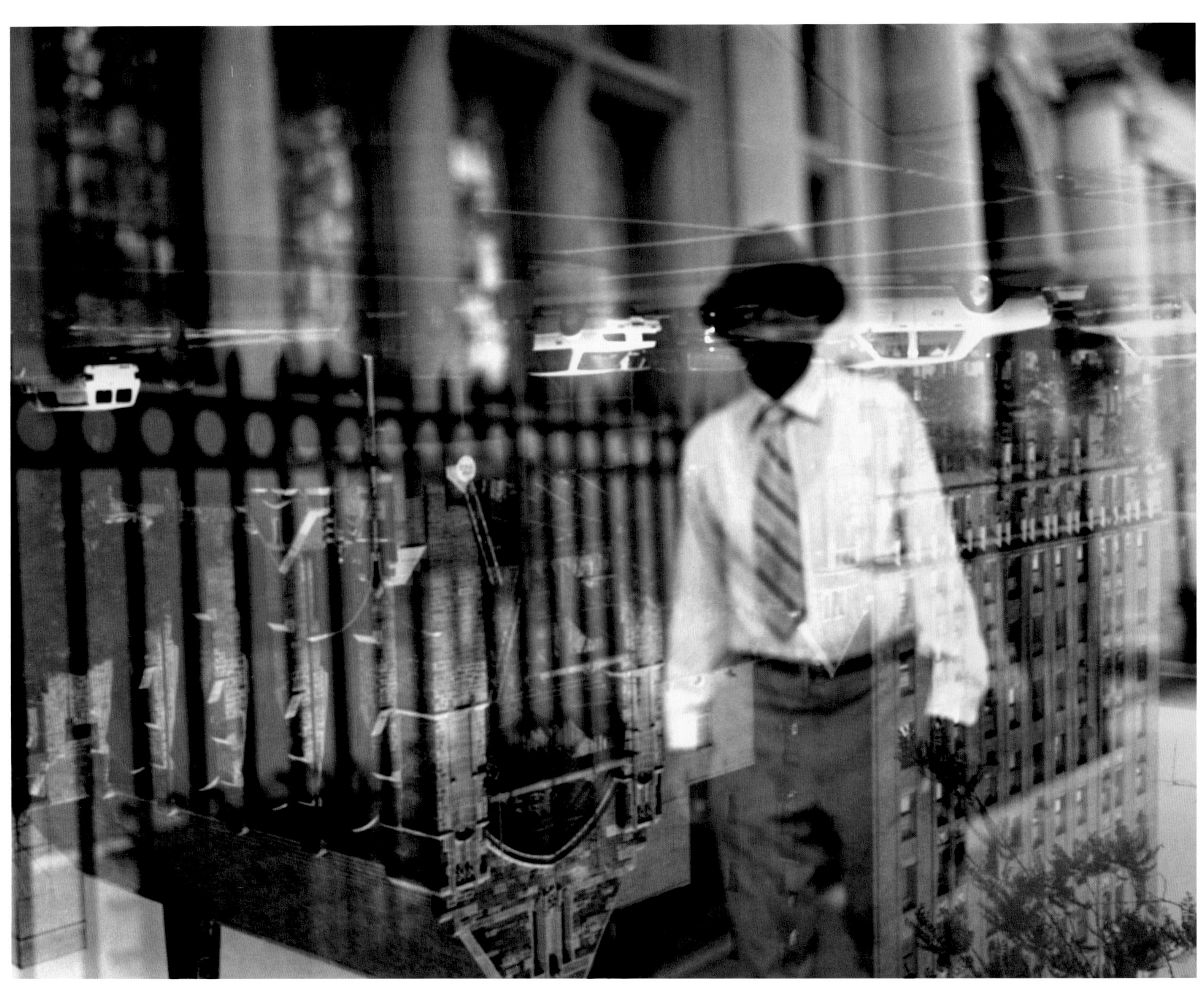

Black Man with Hub Cap Eye. 1992

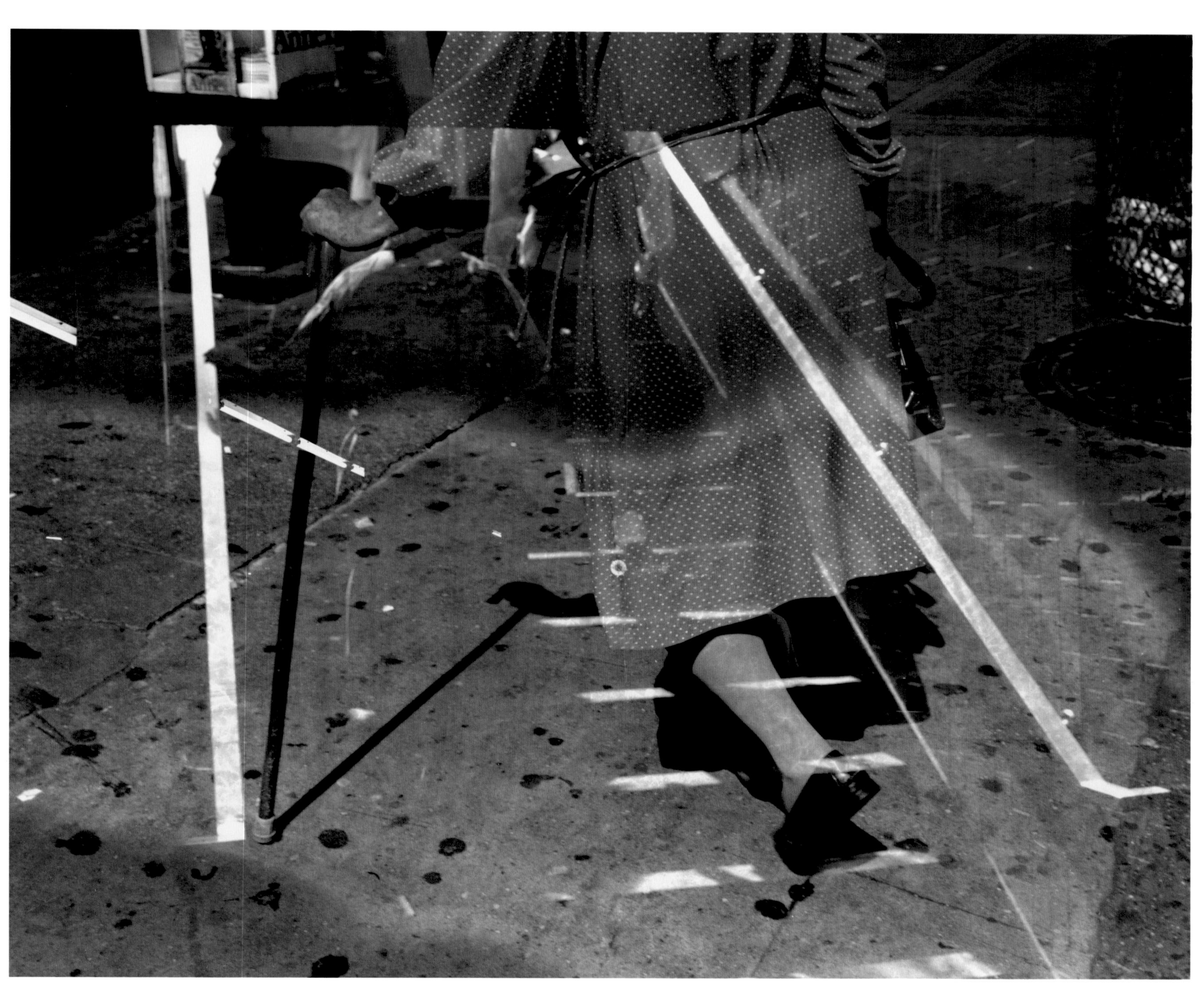

Woman with Cane. 1992

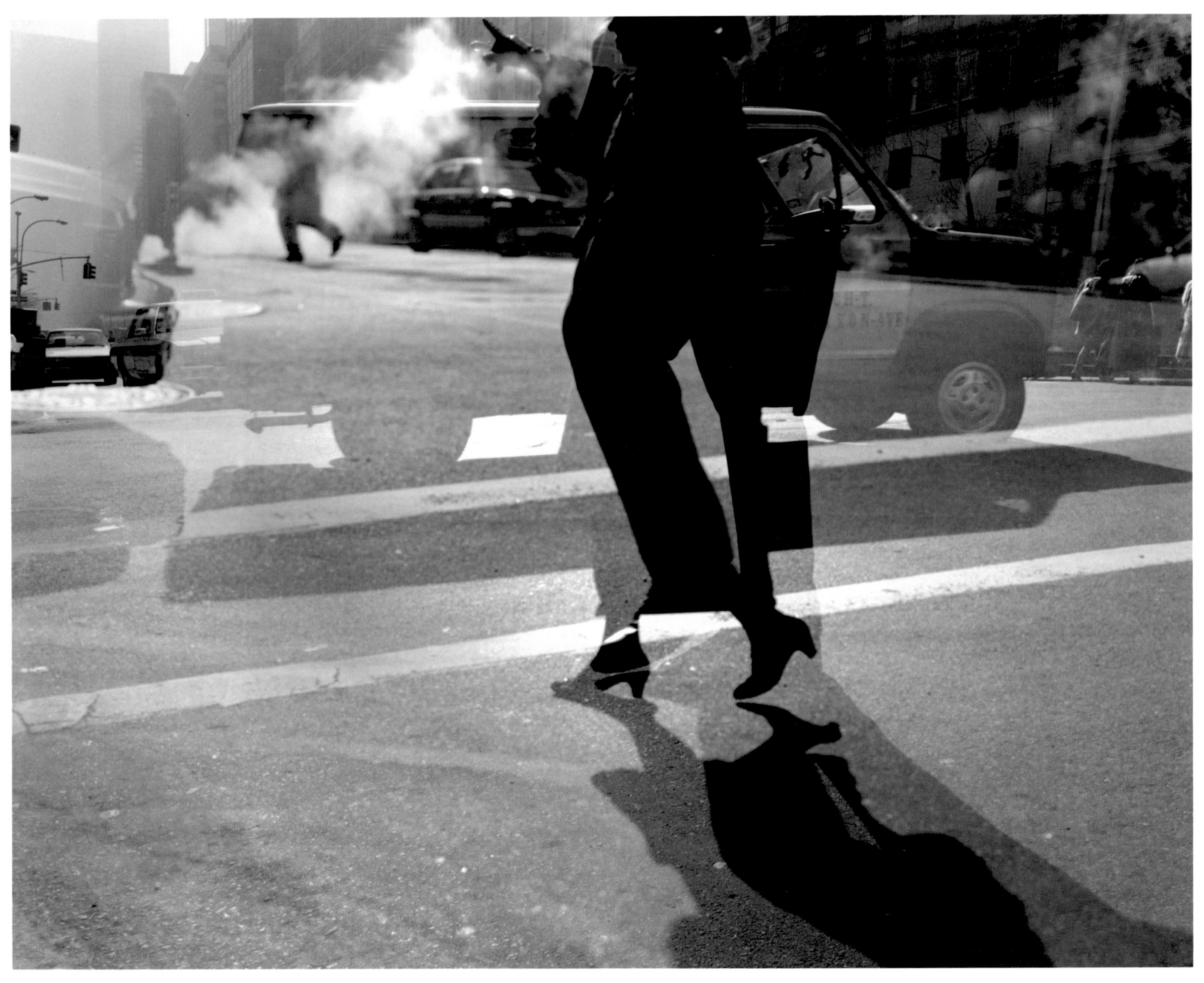

Taxi! 1991

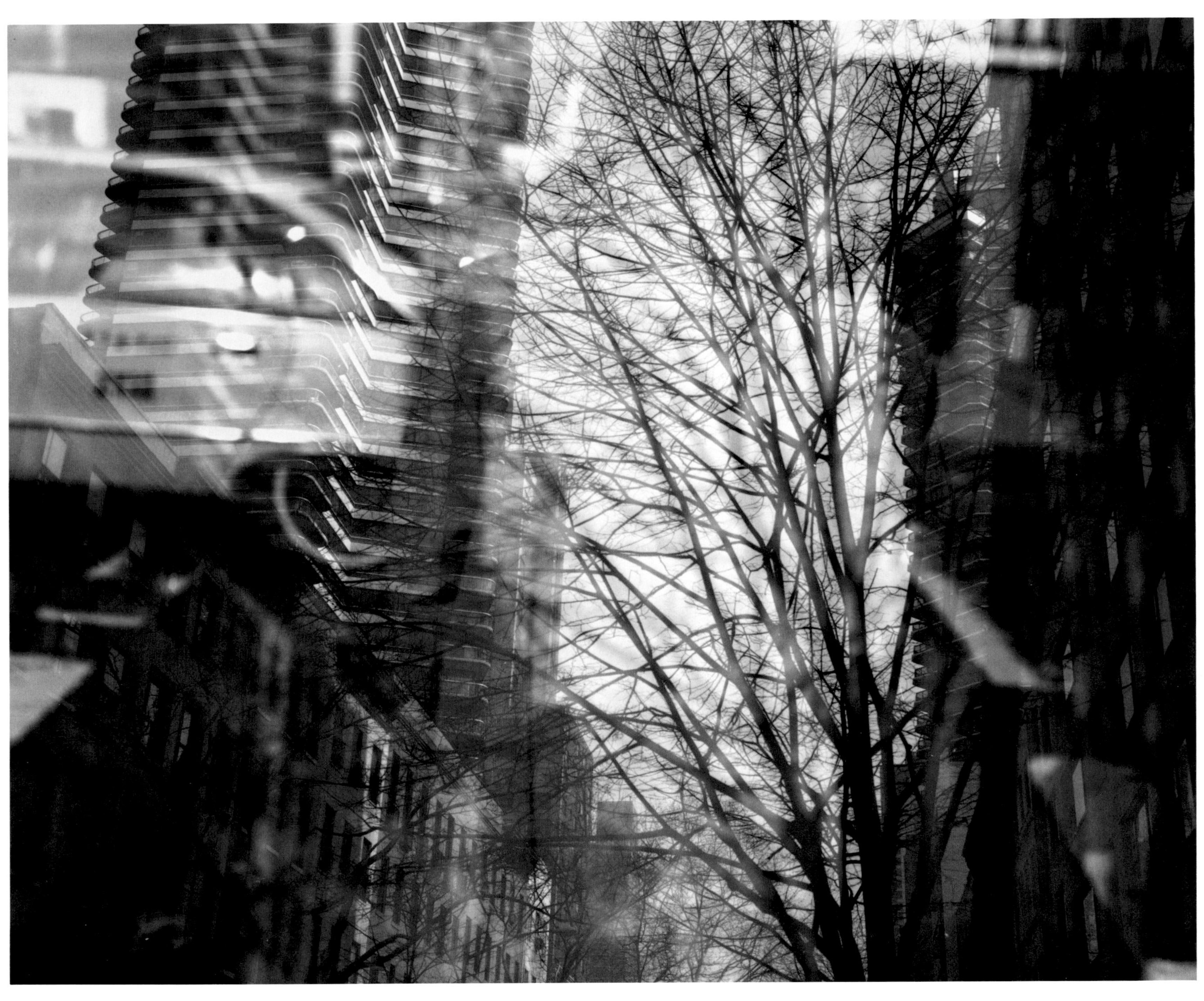

Tree and Taxi in the Sky. 1992

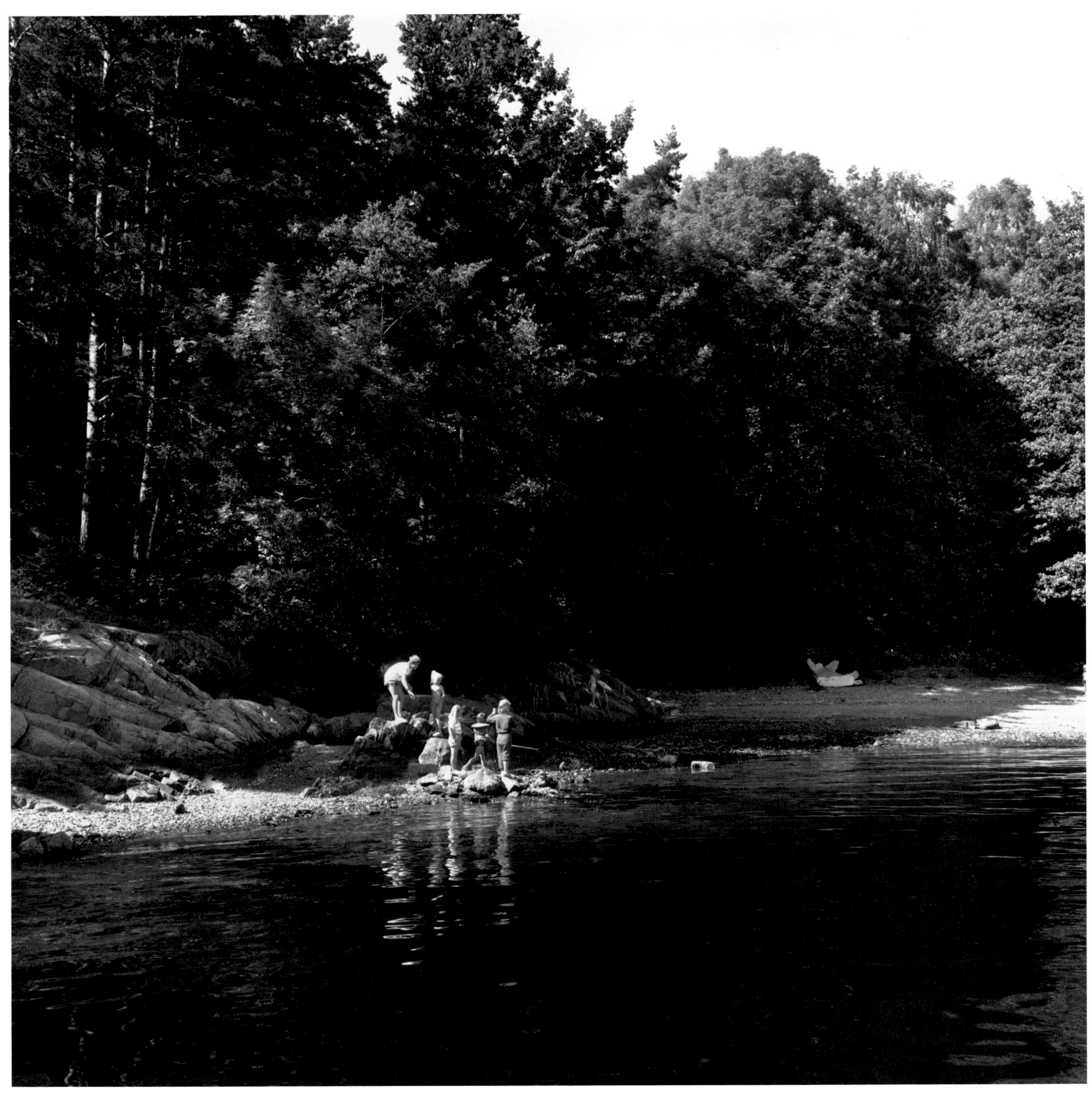

Crabfishing, Haaoeya. 1989

Summer Light

1979-1994

Summer Light

Where does that little orb of sorrow come from at nightfall after a summer's day in the North? It lies there, like a croquet ball in the grass.

The northern summer is so short, and so light that it has become a synonym for paradise—where people dwell. Everything is subject to this light, which is silvery-pale, and at the frayed ends of the day very brittle. Something of that brittleness is carried far into the self-confident days of high summer. In the North, light does not mean a day's work, but just the opposite, play and repose. Summer light is something to take advantage of. It is something that vanishes.

Dag Alveng's pictures of summer light take joy as their principle of composition. Perhaps that is why their orderliness is so exquisite and so fragile.

Alveng stands slightly at a distance, so that the woman sunning her breasts while she reads a book is partly hidden by a bough of dark, sweet cherries. He sees how a garden table and a tree both draw curving shadows that contain flashes of sunlight. The chair beside hers is empty. On the table is a pan with a plate for a lid. This moment of harmony will soon be over. Alveng takes another step back and sees the last light of an evening some-where between spring and summer. A little fire is in the garden, and every bud bears a promise that this is only a beginning, a promise that consoles. And the buds have their counterpart in the other things that are opened in the picture: the open door and open windows of the house, the open cellar hatch, and the open bottles of wine. Even the back of the car is open!

And Alveng moves even further away, so that foliage draws black lace patterns on the boys who are playing croquet. It is as though he were seeing a stage, from the other side: a single moment of perfection, of which the players themselves are unaware.

In spite of this redeeming light and this summer idyll, there is nothing sentimental about Dag Alveng's photographs. Perhaps this is due to the fact that he does not set things right. The washing-up brush in the plastic bowl has a black hair entangled in it, and the light that is reflected in the grimy water surface comes from a naked light bulb. The garden chair in the enchanting spring garden is of the simplest design and has large stains. And the shady, broad-leaf trees in the landscape stand between bare slabs of rock. This paradise is democratic rather than universal.

And this paradise is dependent on the photographer's temperament. Here he, too, stands, naked except for gumshoes, brandishing a remote control release, about to dive into the sea. The act looks extremely dangerous, especially when we think of how close to the surface the seaweed is. But the event makes for a perfect picture.

So, where does that little orb of sorrow come from right in the middle of summer? Perhaps from the knowledge that this perfection depends on our being able to experience it, and on our being able to hold onto it, for just a moment.

Gertrud Sandqvist

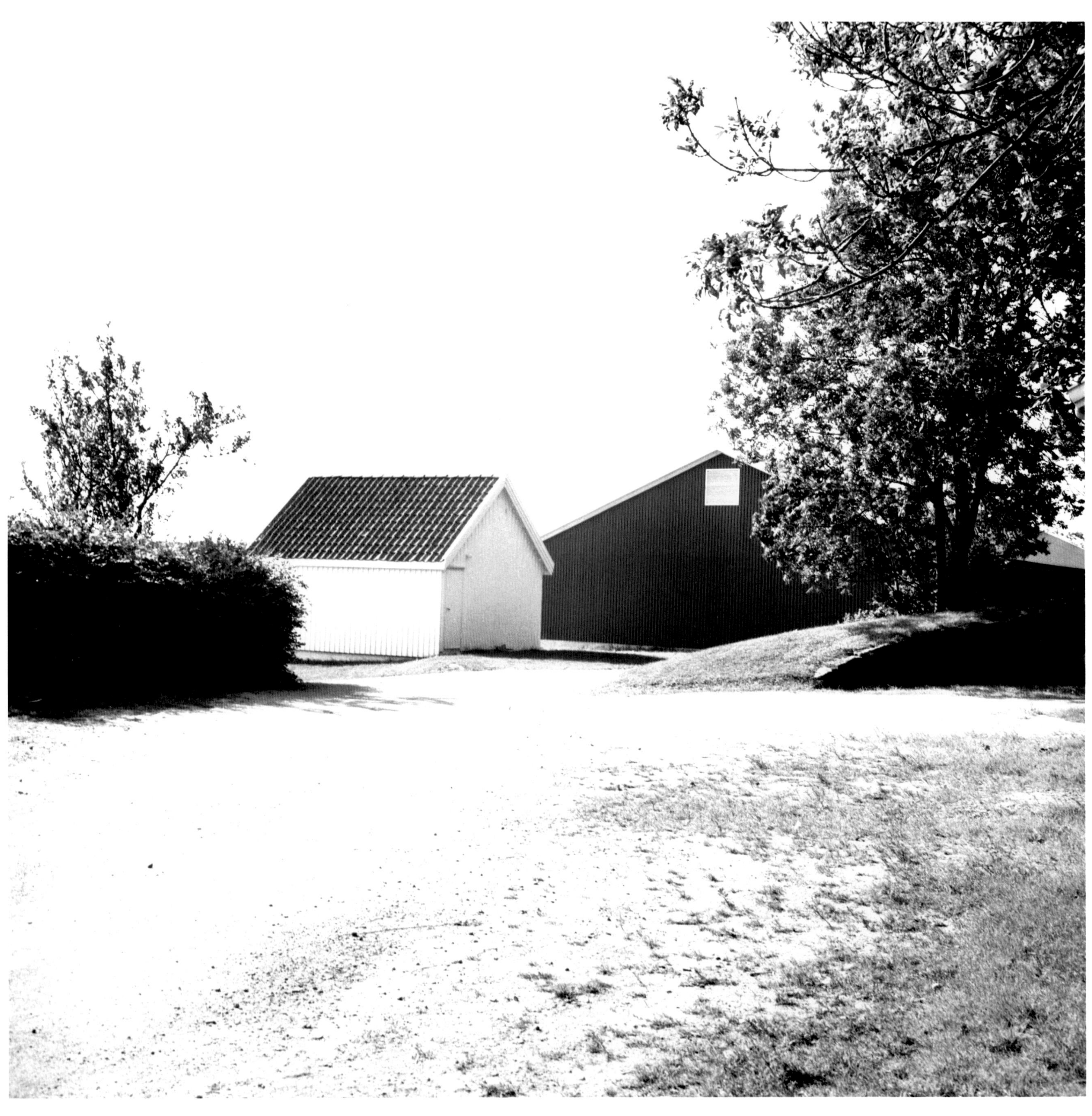

Small White House and Barn, Hvasser, 1980

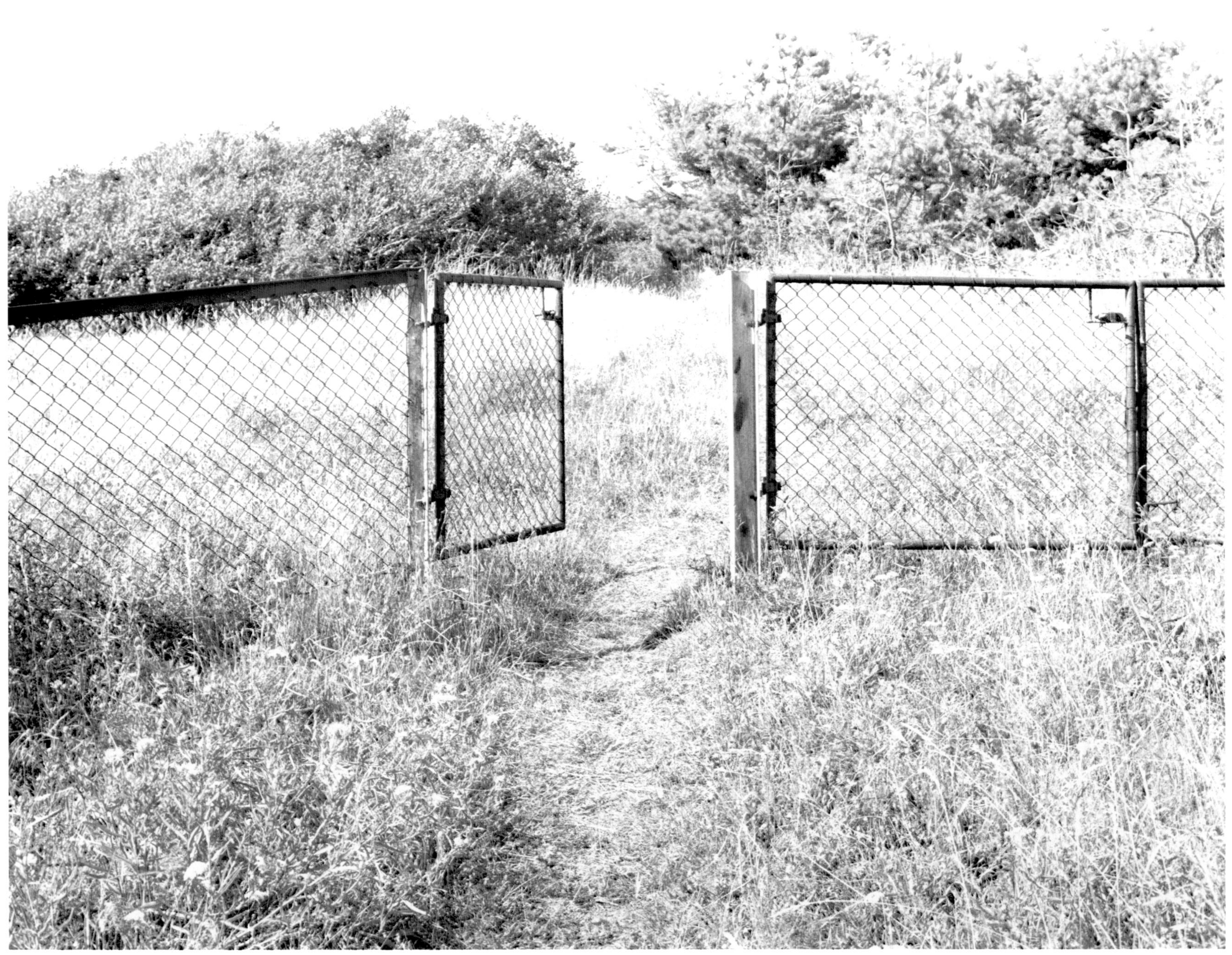

Open Gate, Hvasser. 1979

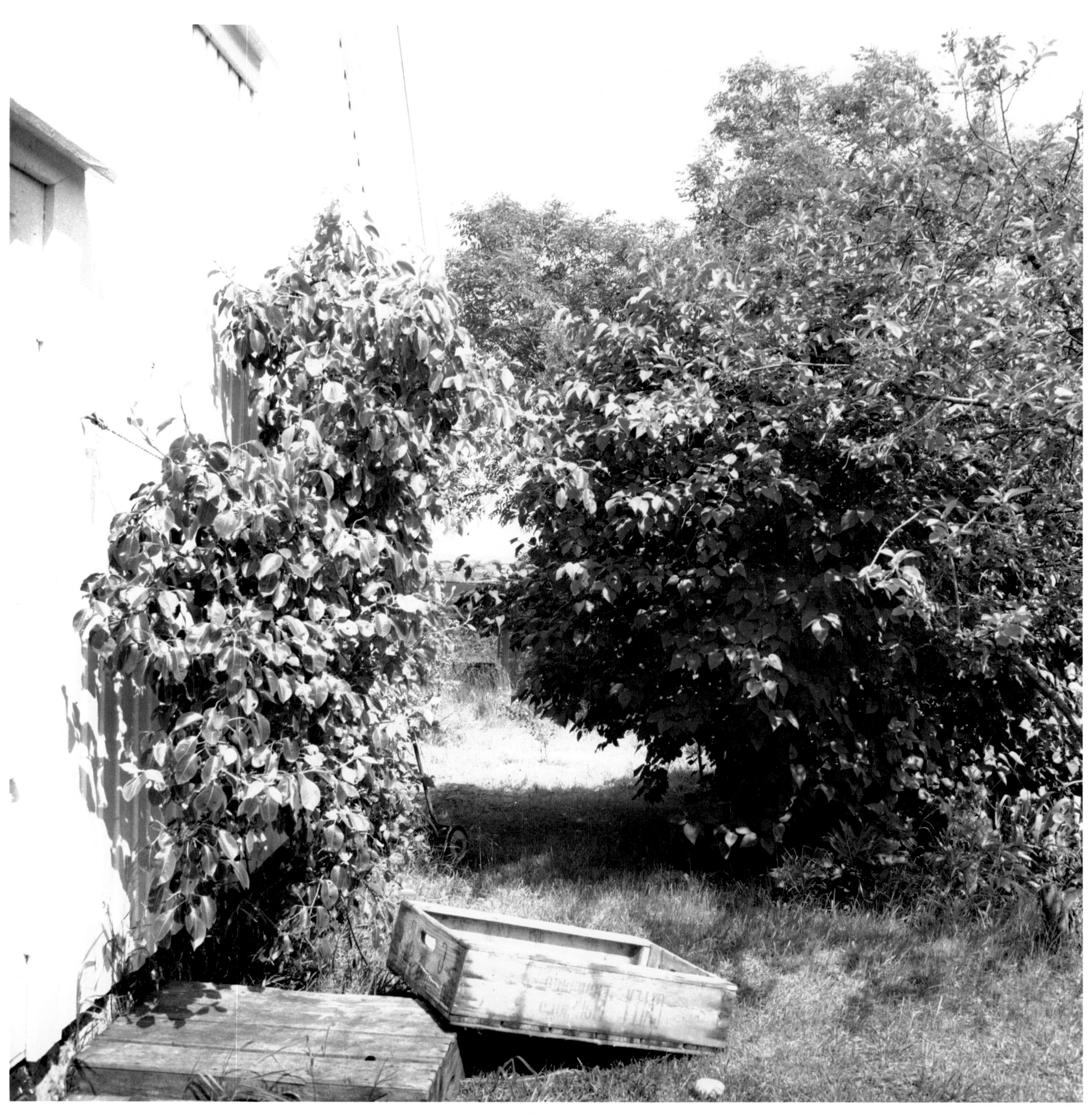

Crate, Hvasser. 1987

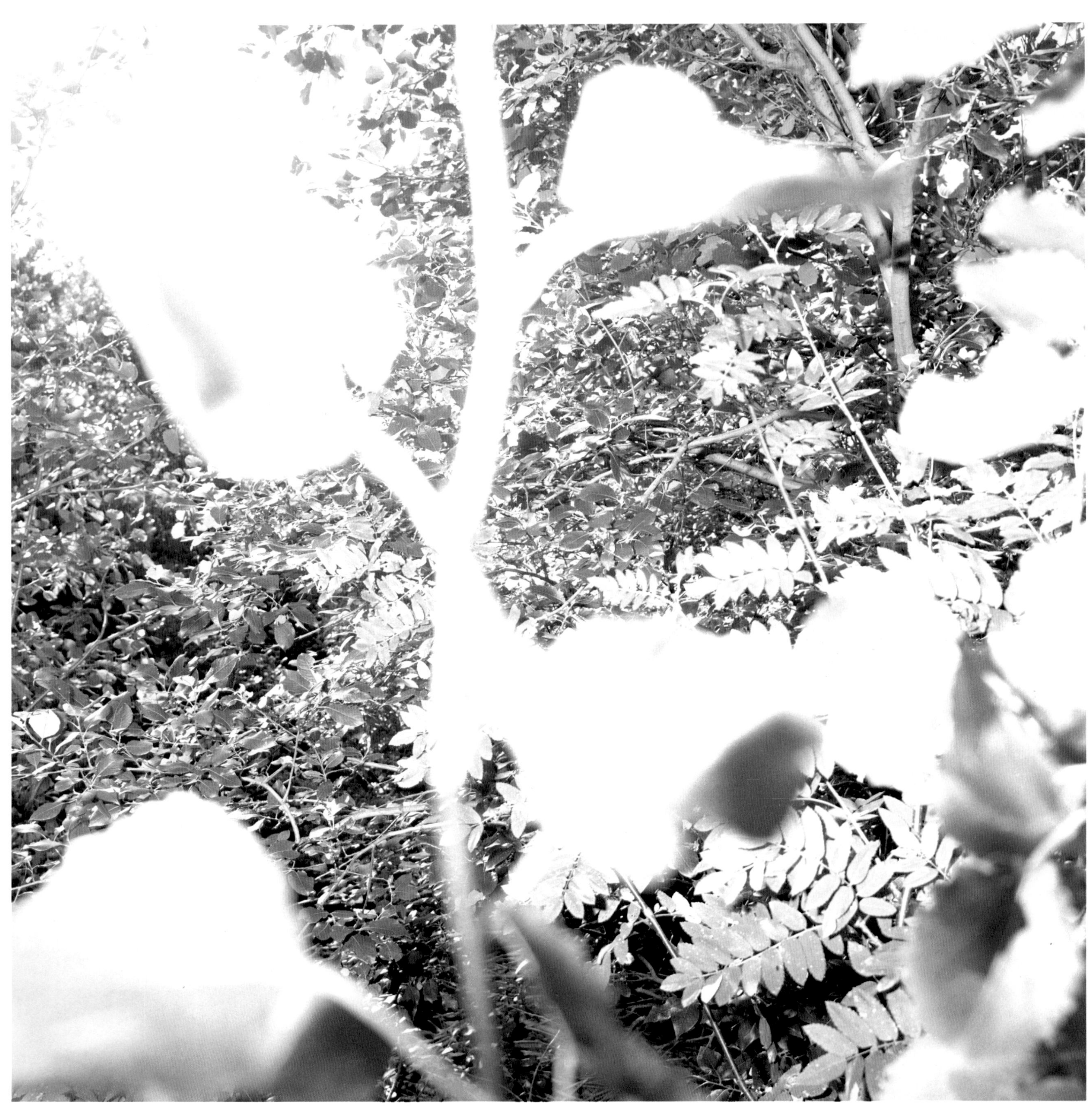

Bleak Flowers, Hvasser, 1980

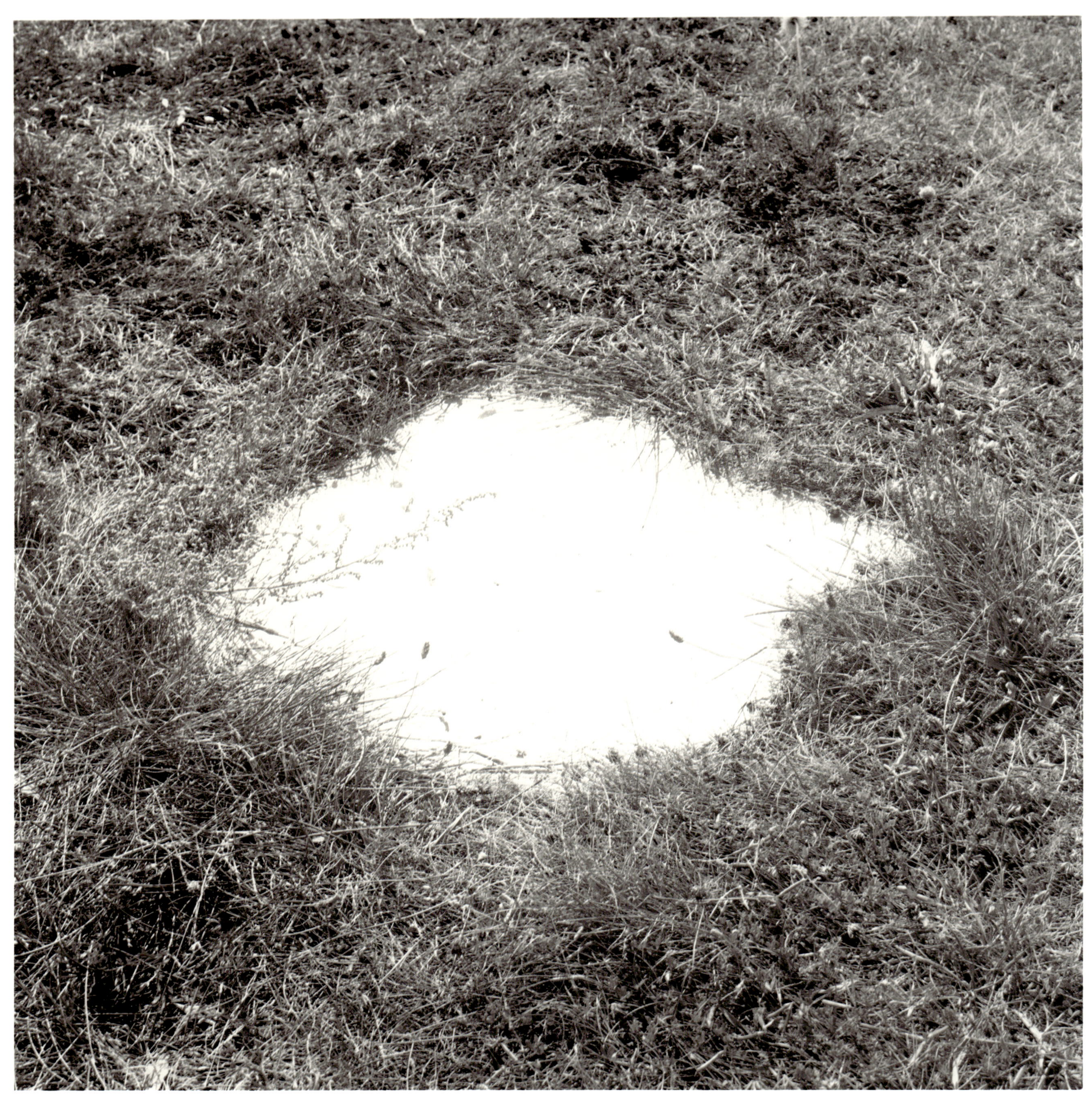

Slate, Hvasser, 1980

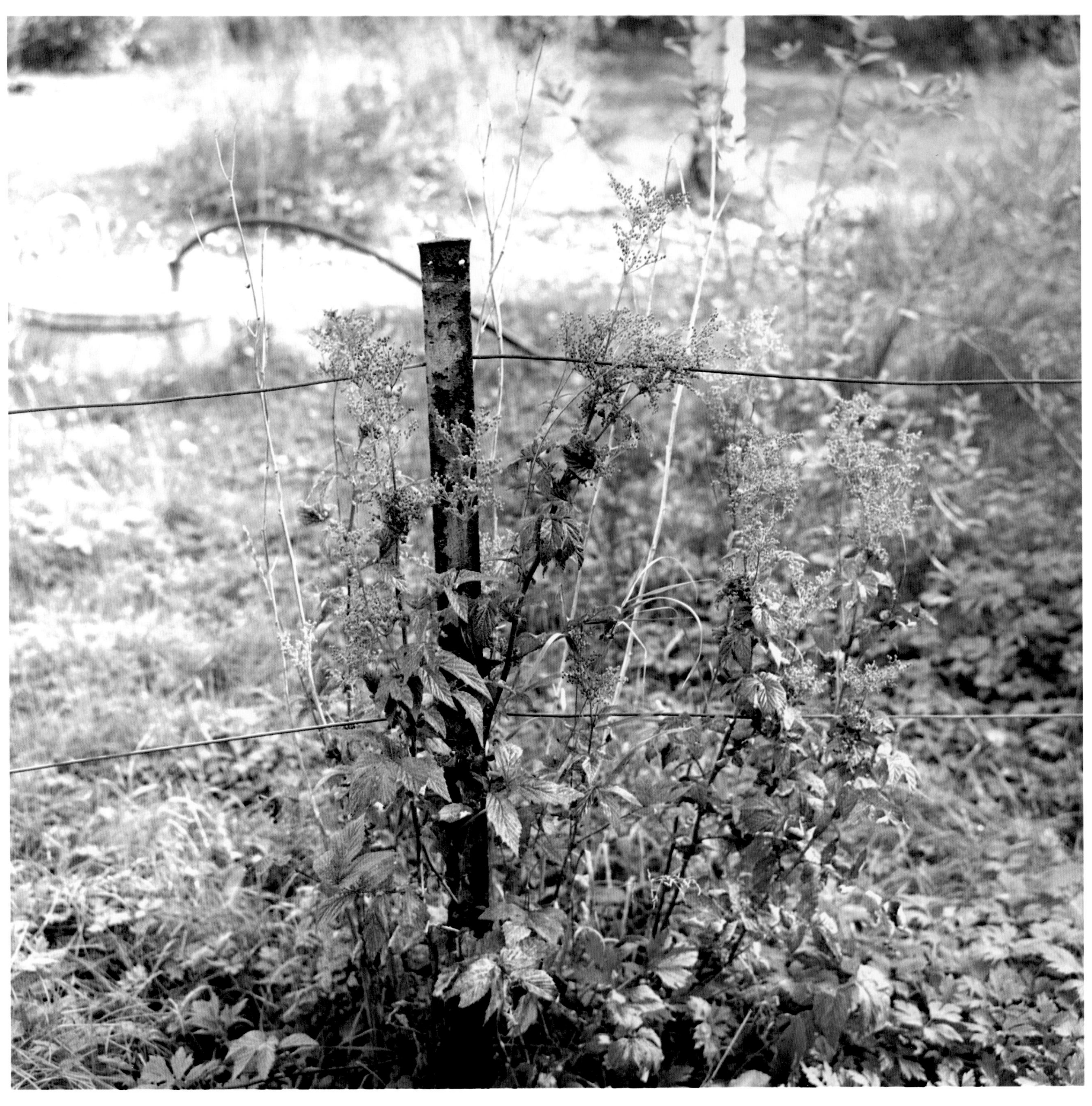

Fencepost, Hvasser. 1987

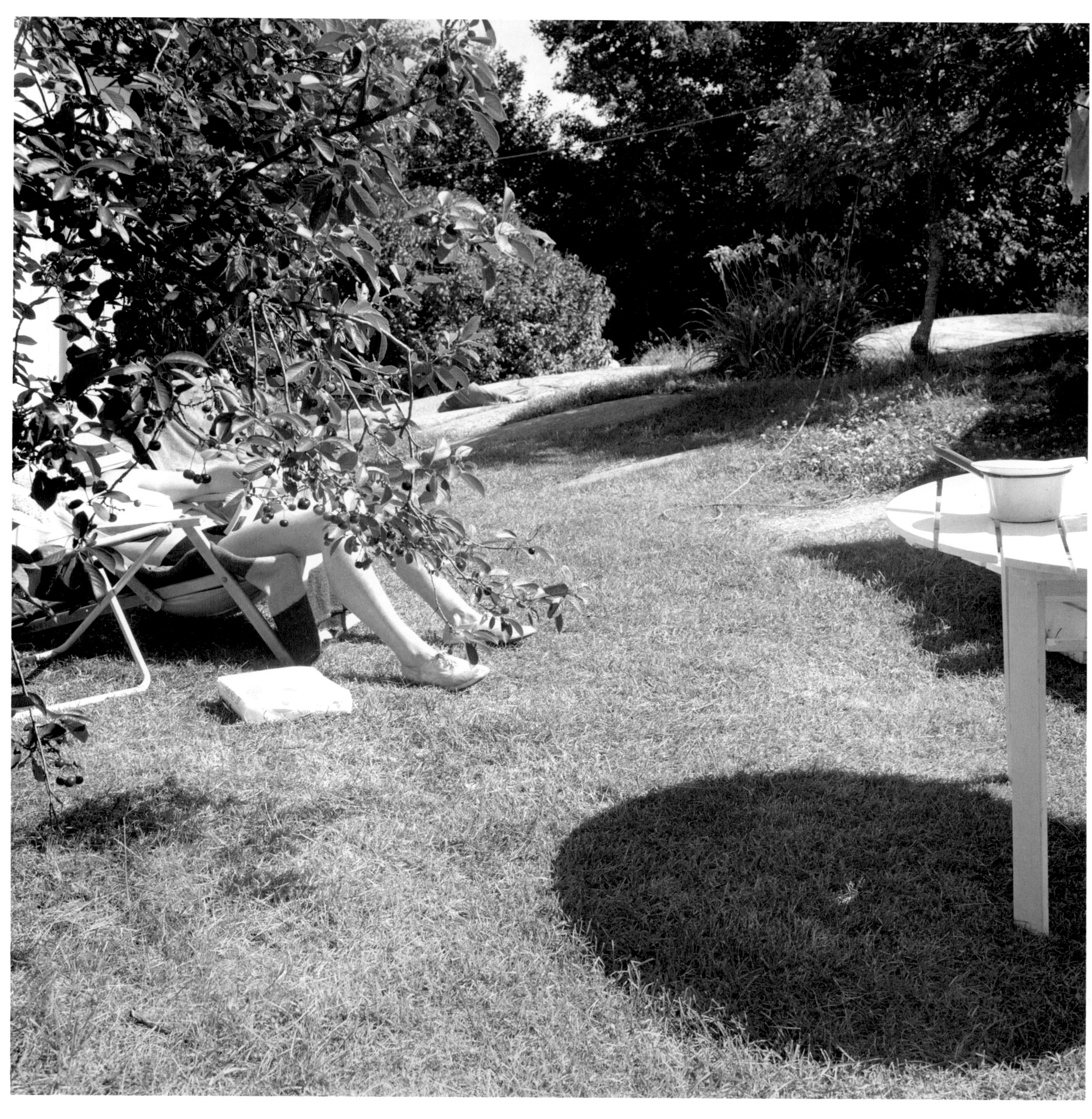

Cherries. Hvasser. 1981

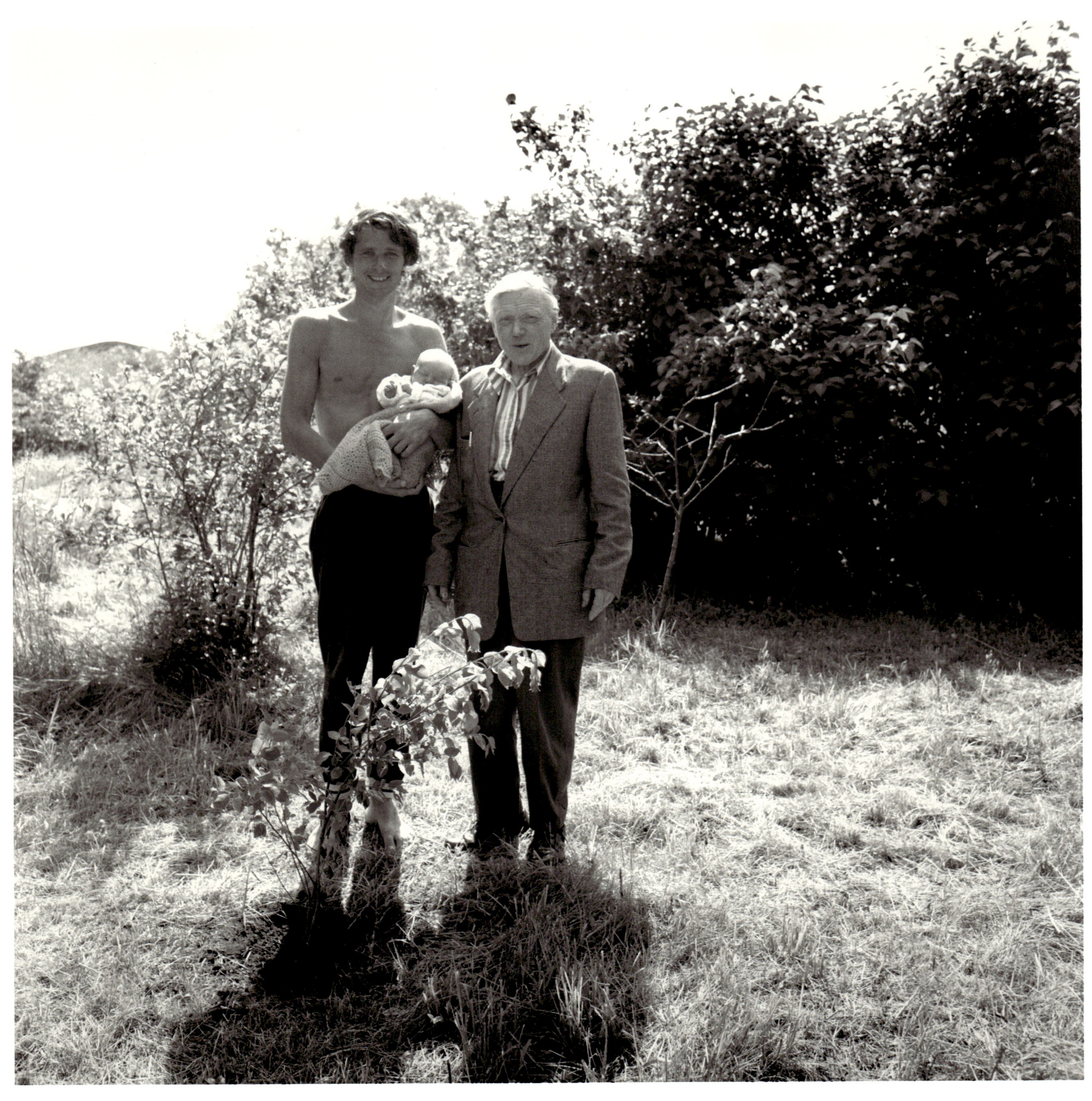

Dugald, Oscar, and Mathilda (no. 1), Hvasser. 1987

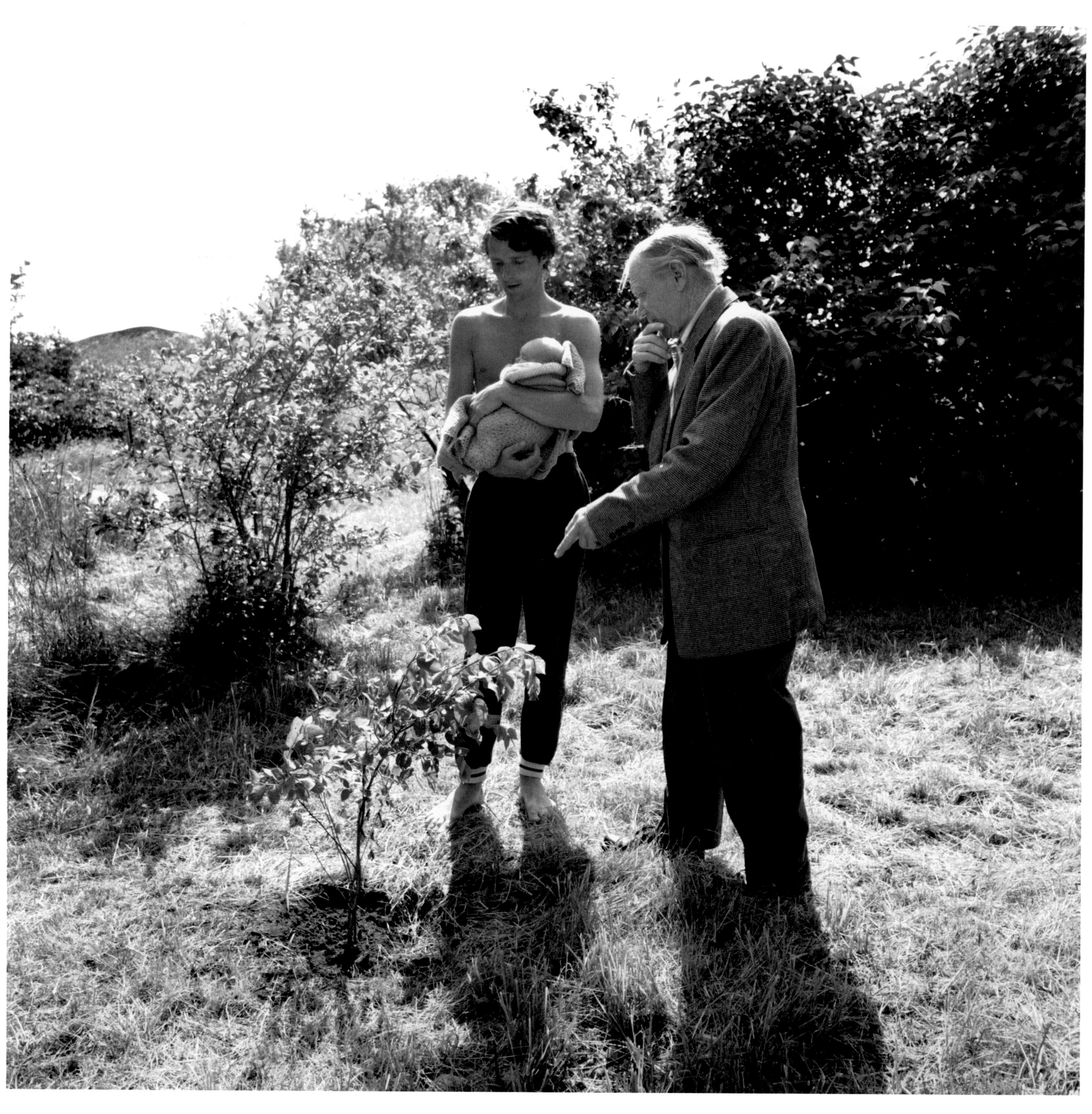

Dugald, Oscar, and Mathilda (no. 2), Hvasser. 1987

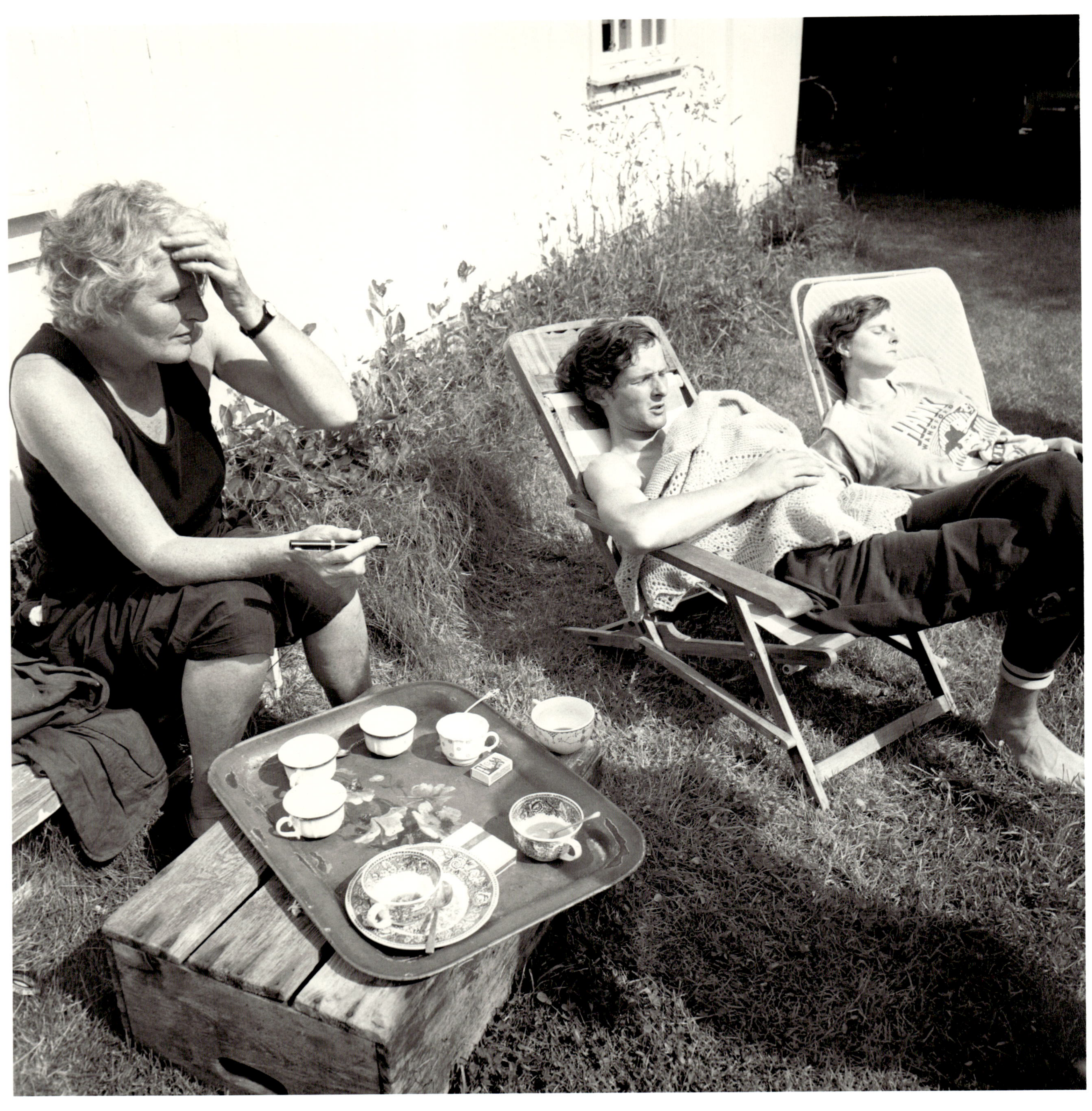

Maureen, Dugald, and Kirsti, Hvasser. 1987

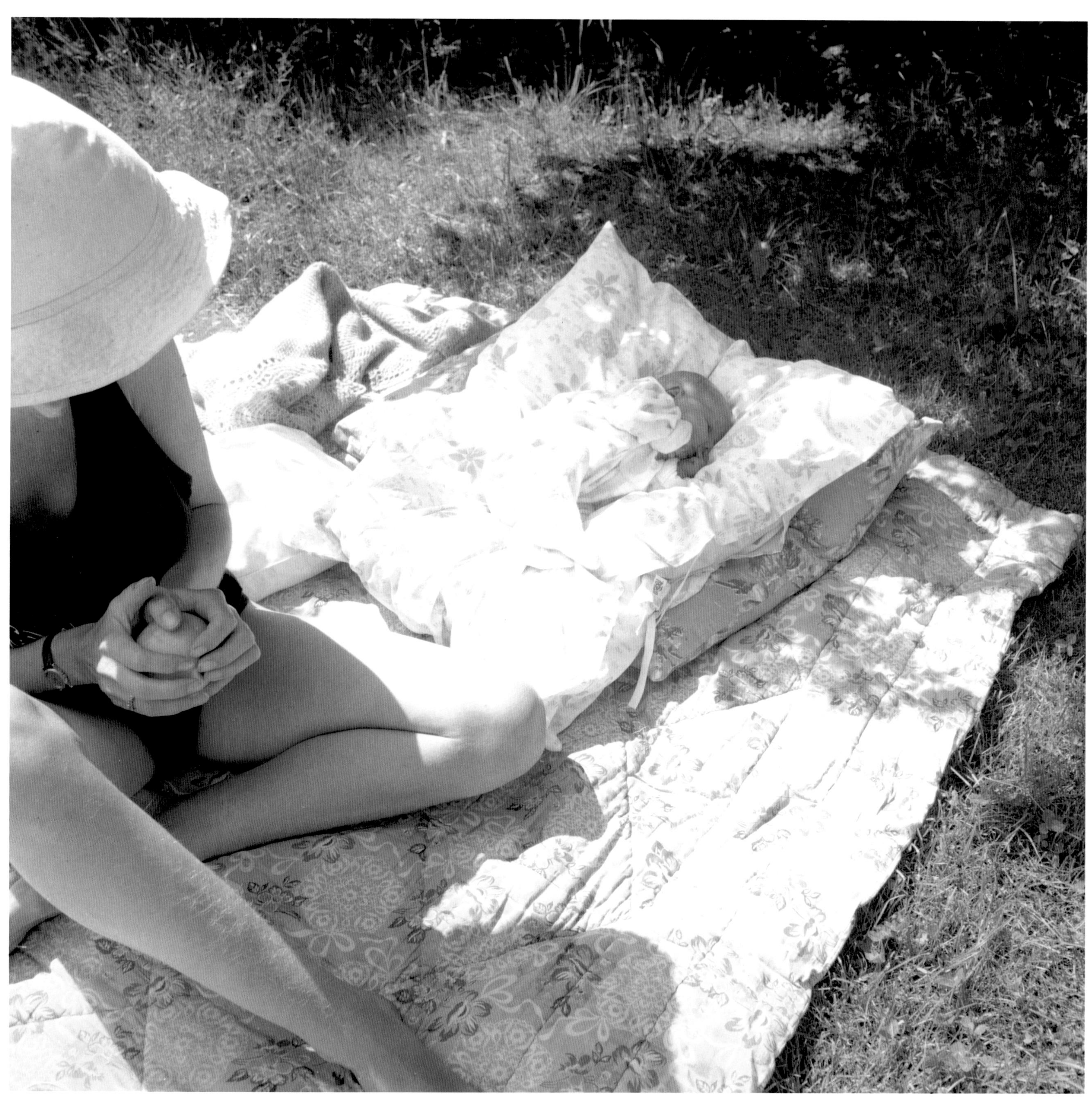

Beth and Mathilda, Hvasser. 1987

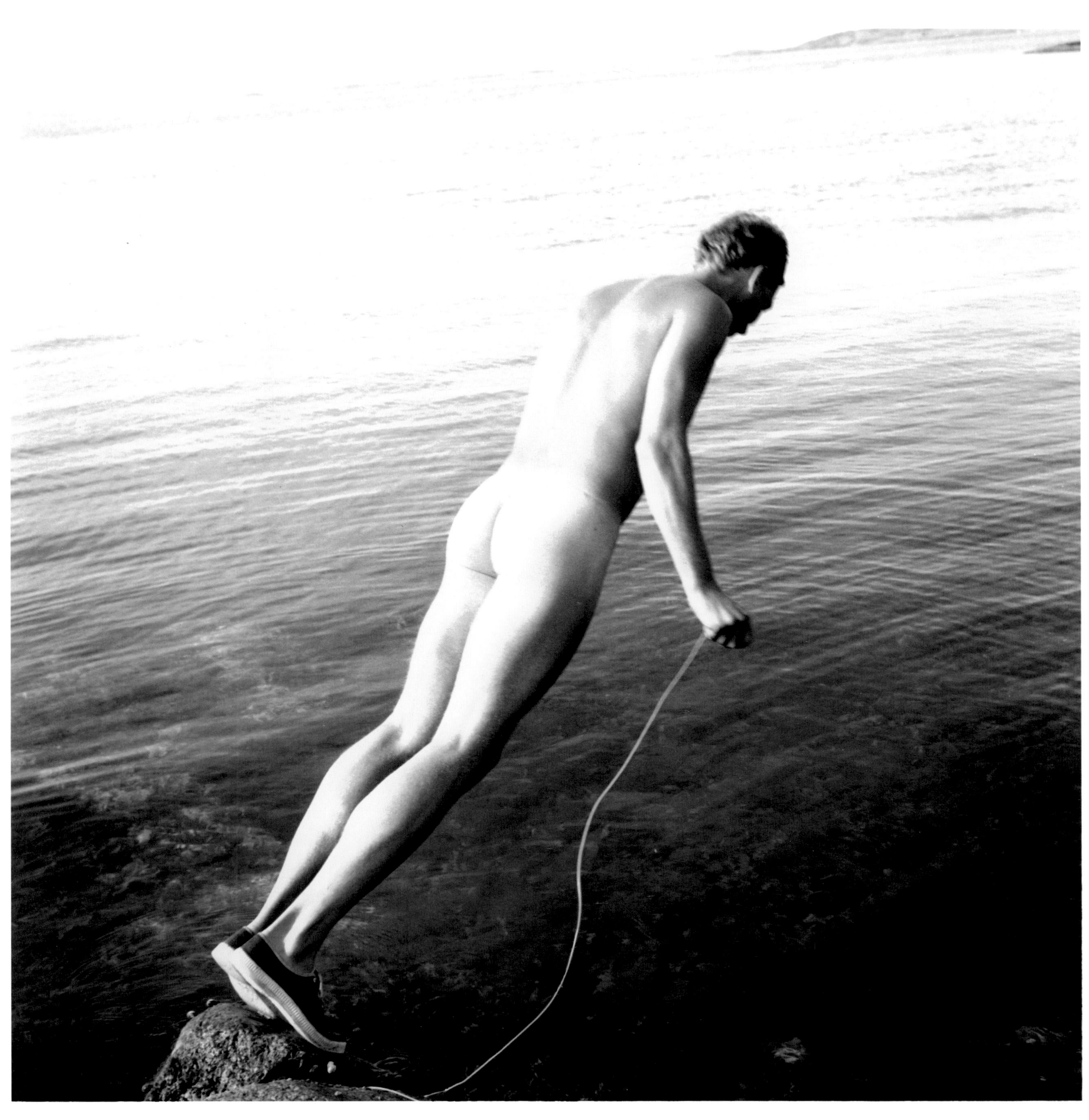

The Photographer Shoots Himself, Hvasser, 1981 (with greetings to Jim Bengston)

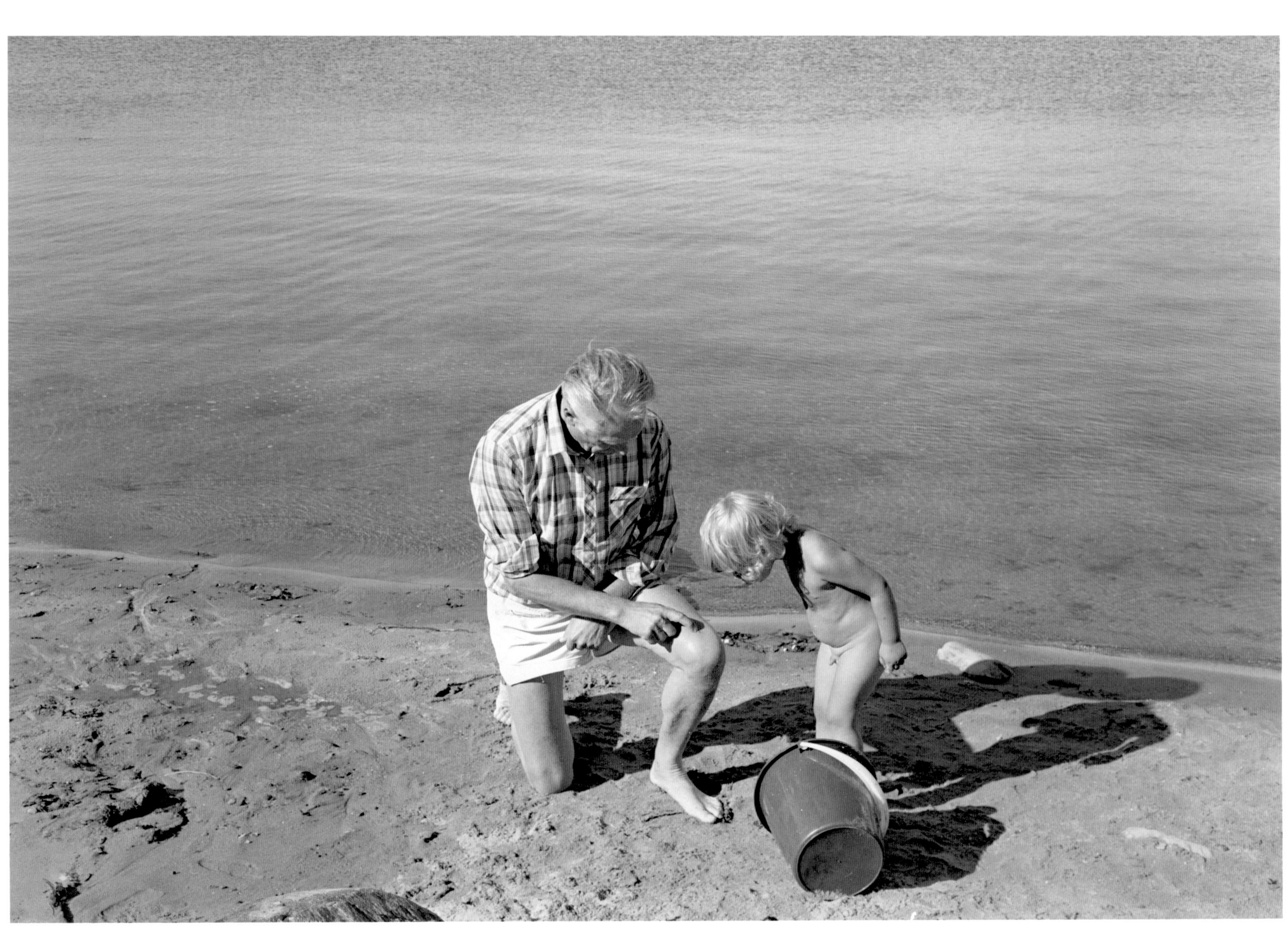

Ladybird , Grandfather, and Karl, Havstensund, 1986

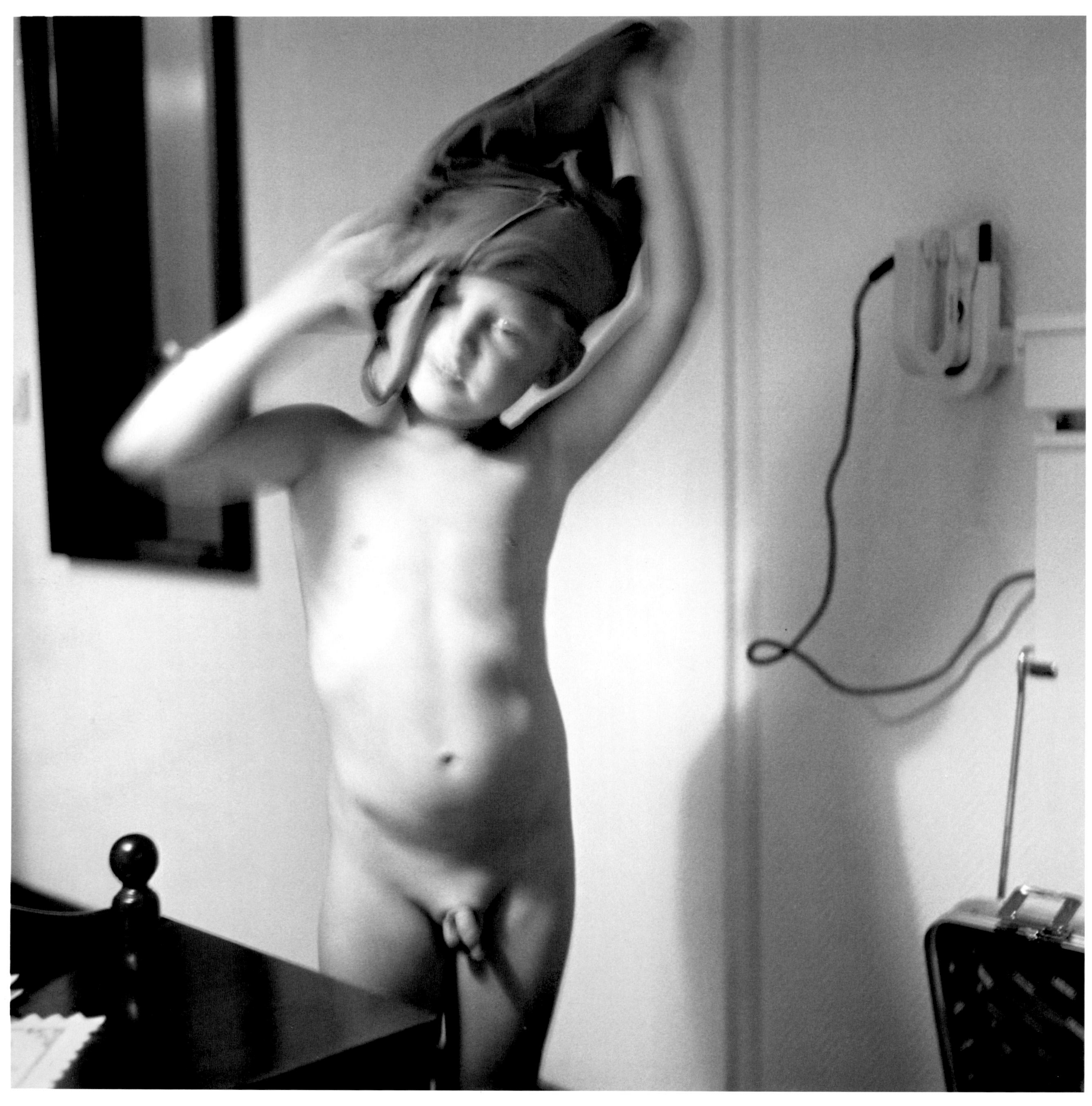

Karl, Hotel Room, Göthenborg. 1988

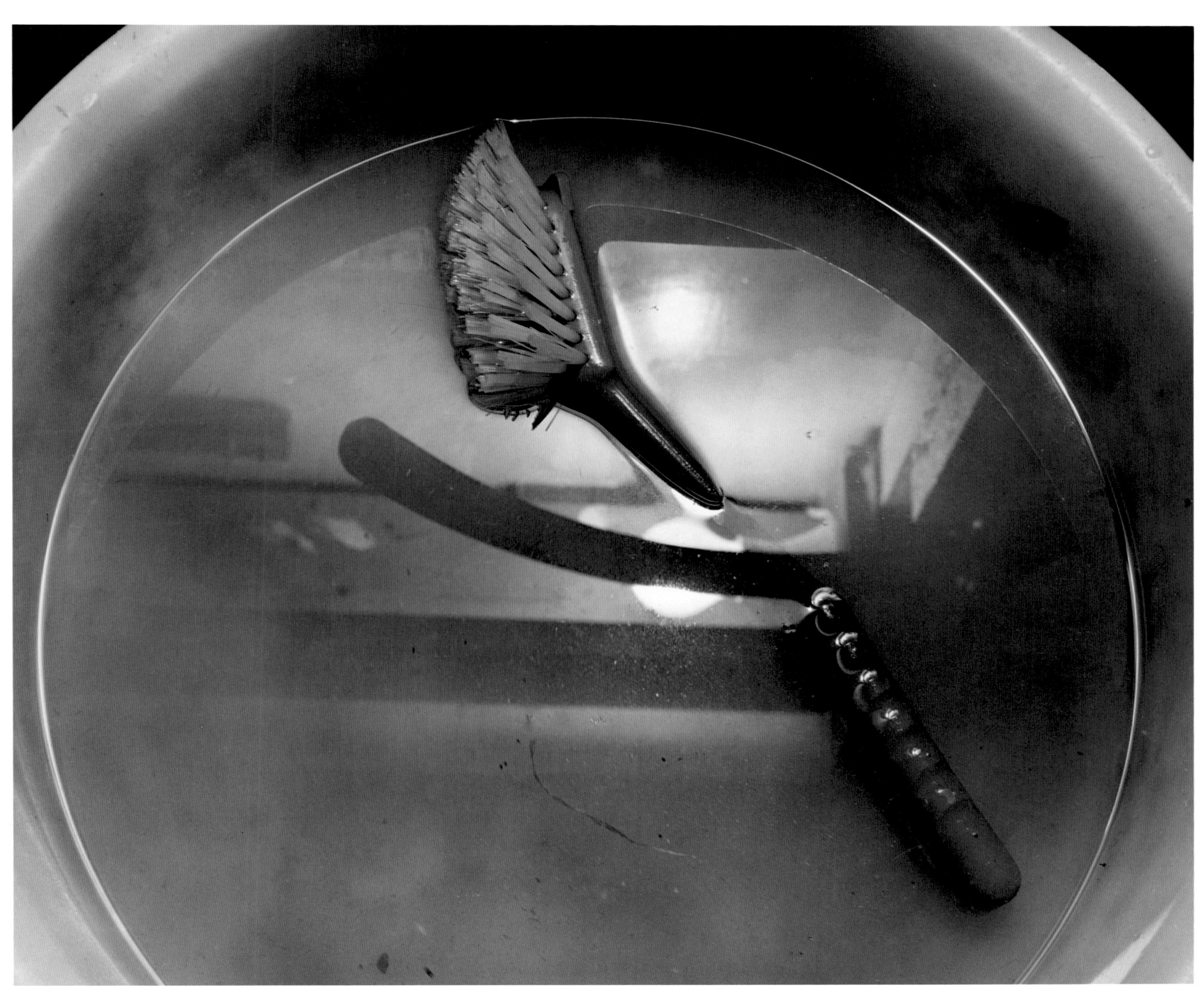

Dish Brush, Hvasser. 1981

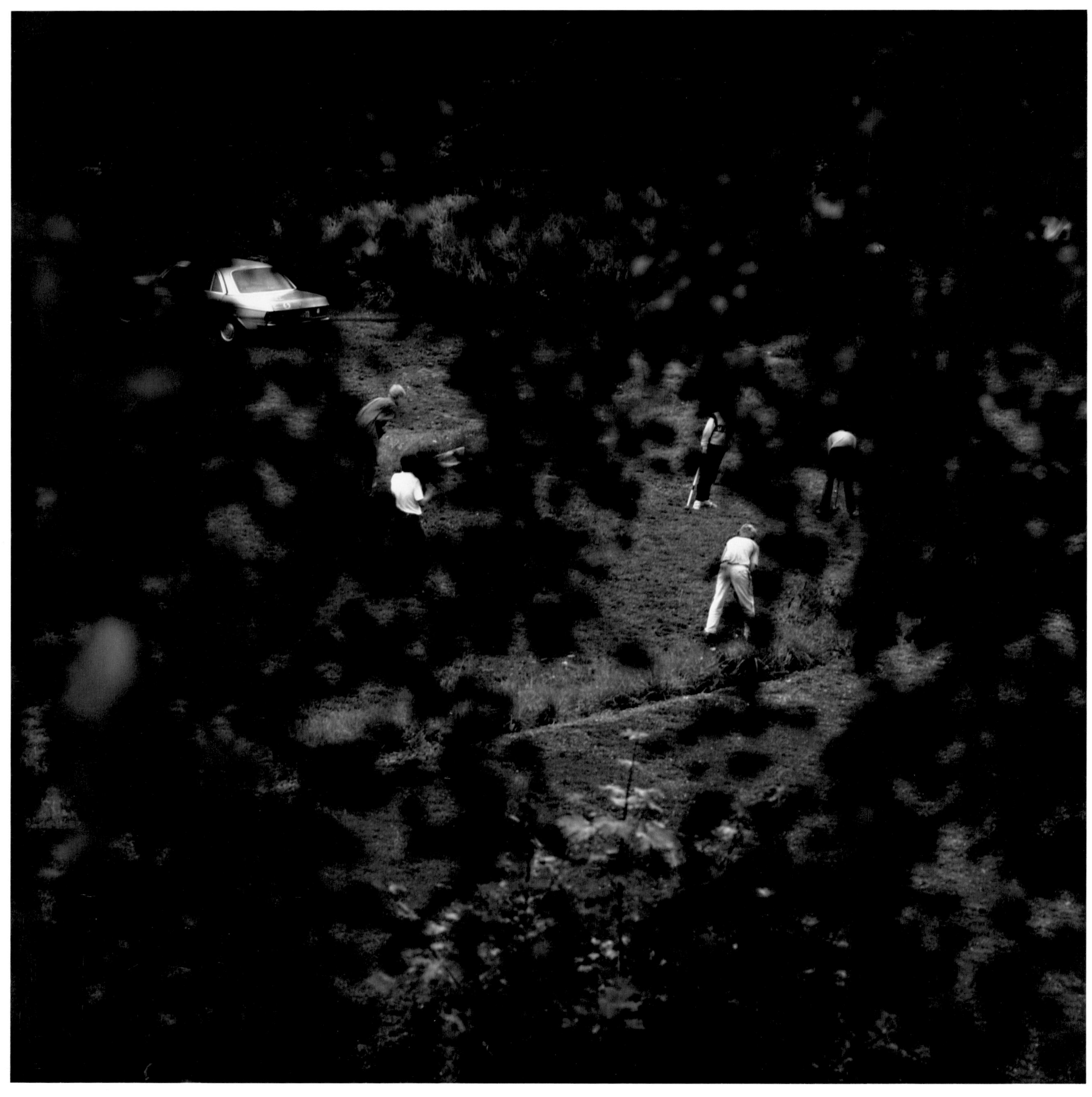

Playing Croquet, Holmsbu. 1985

France

1980

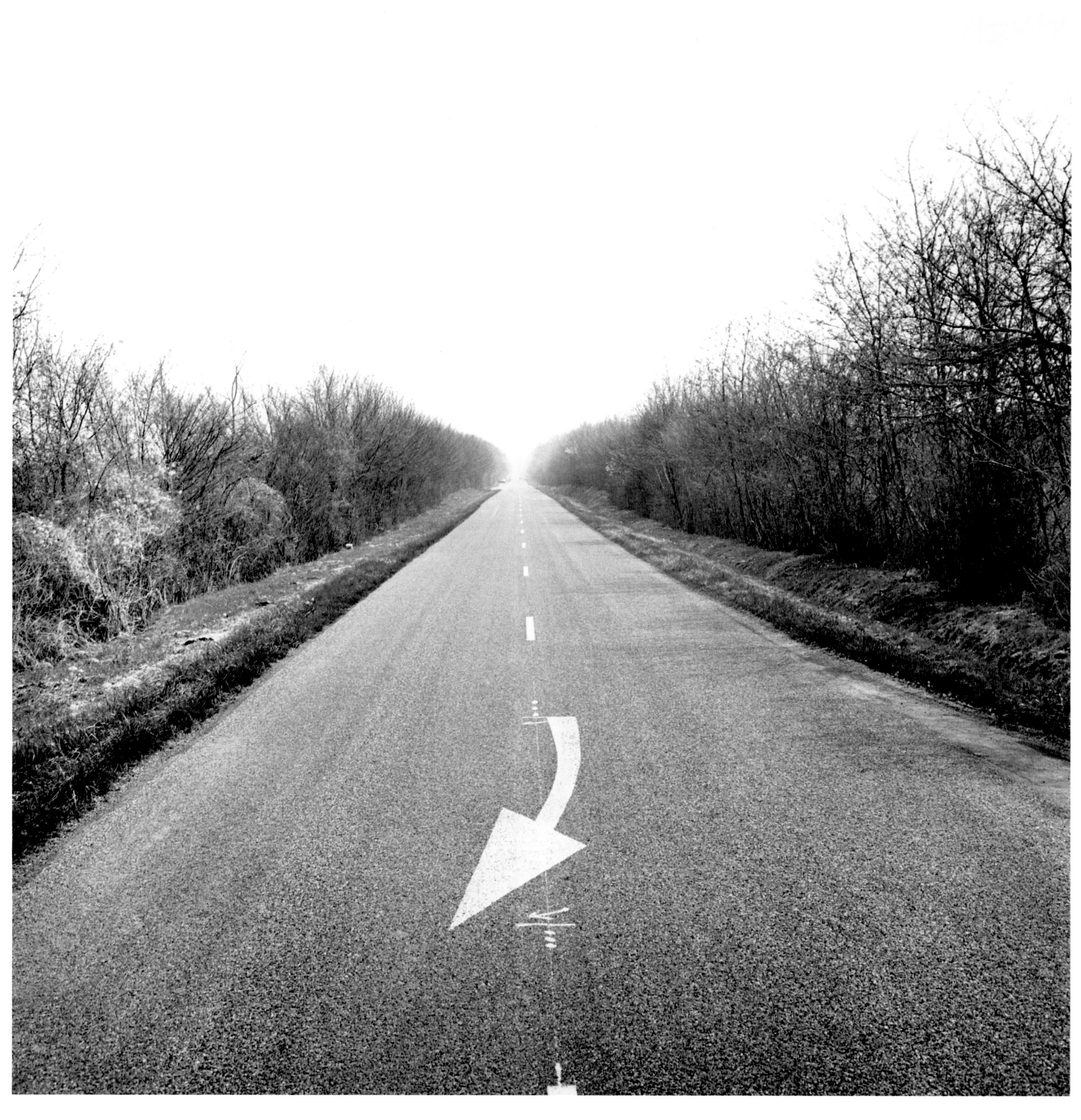

Arrow, Bourgogne. 1980

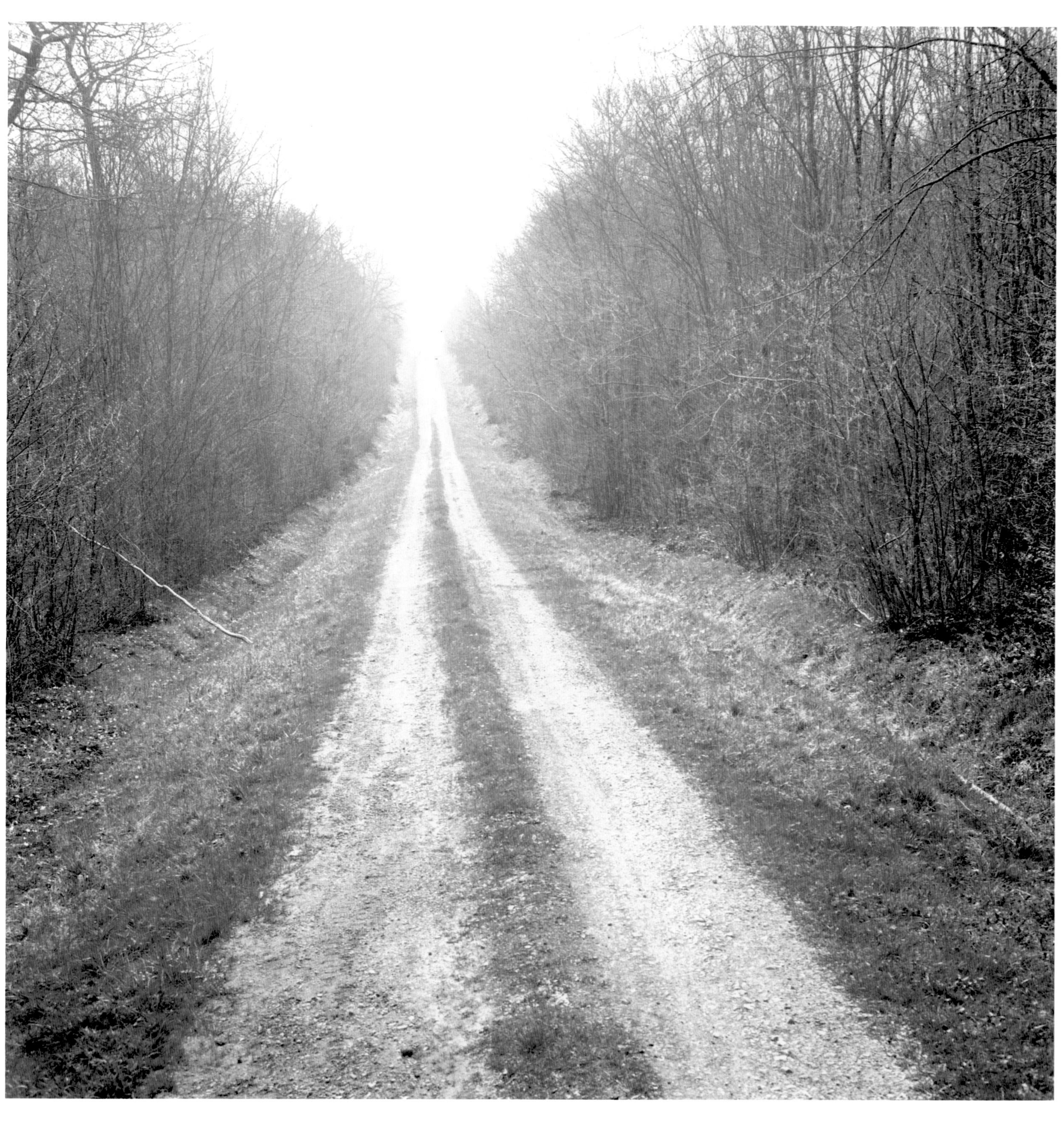

Sideroad, Bourgogne. 1980

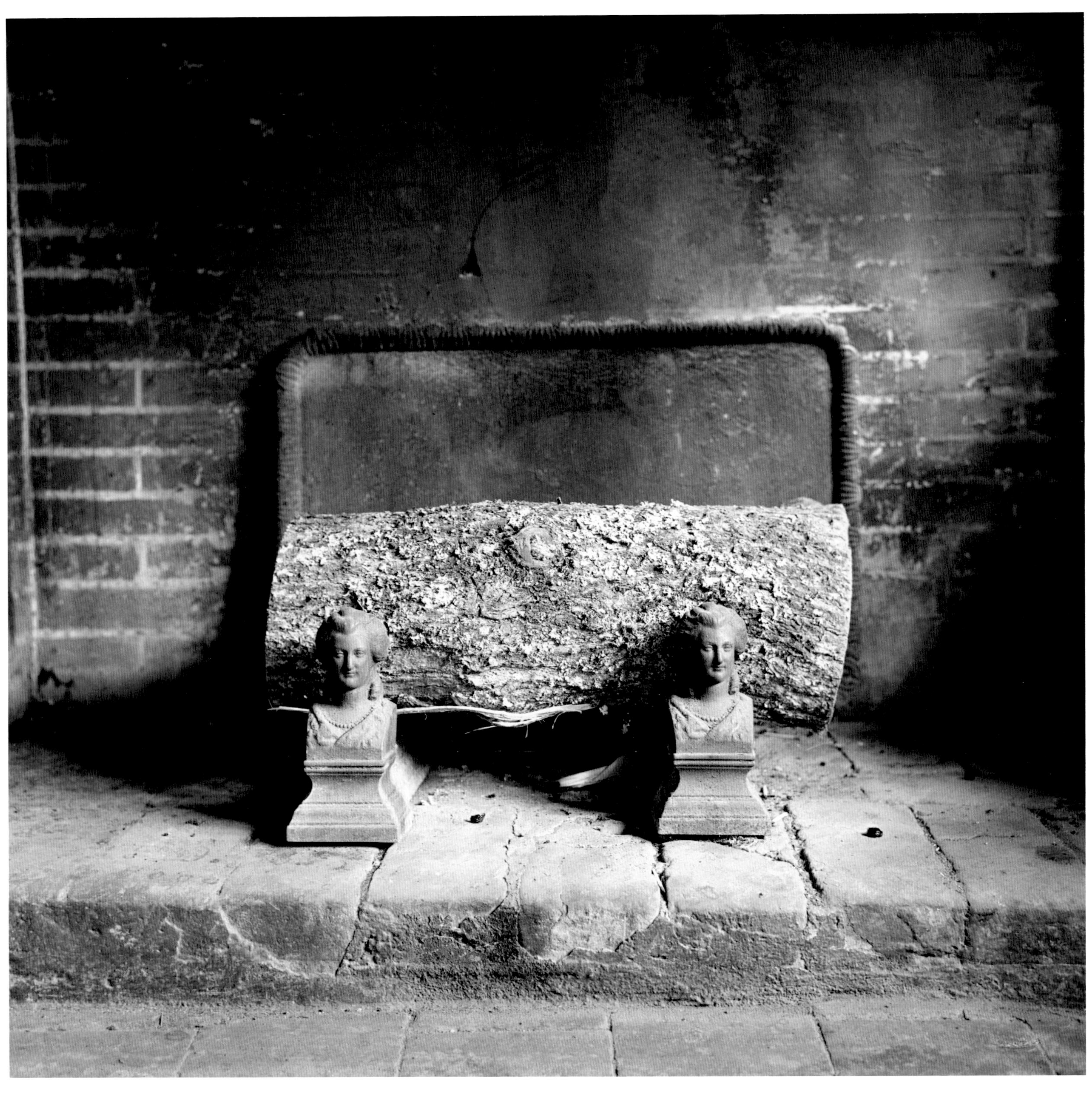

Fireplace I, Bourgogne. 1980

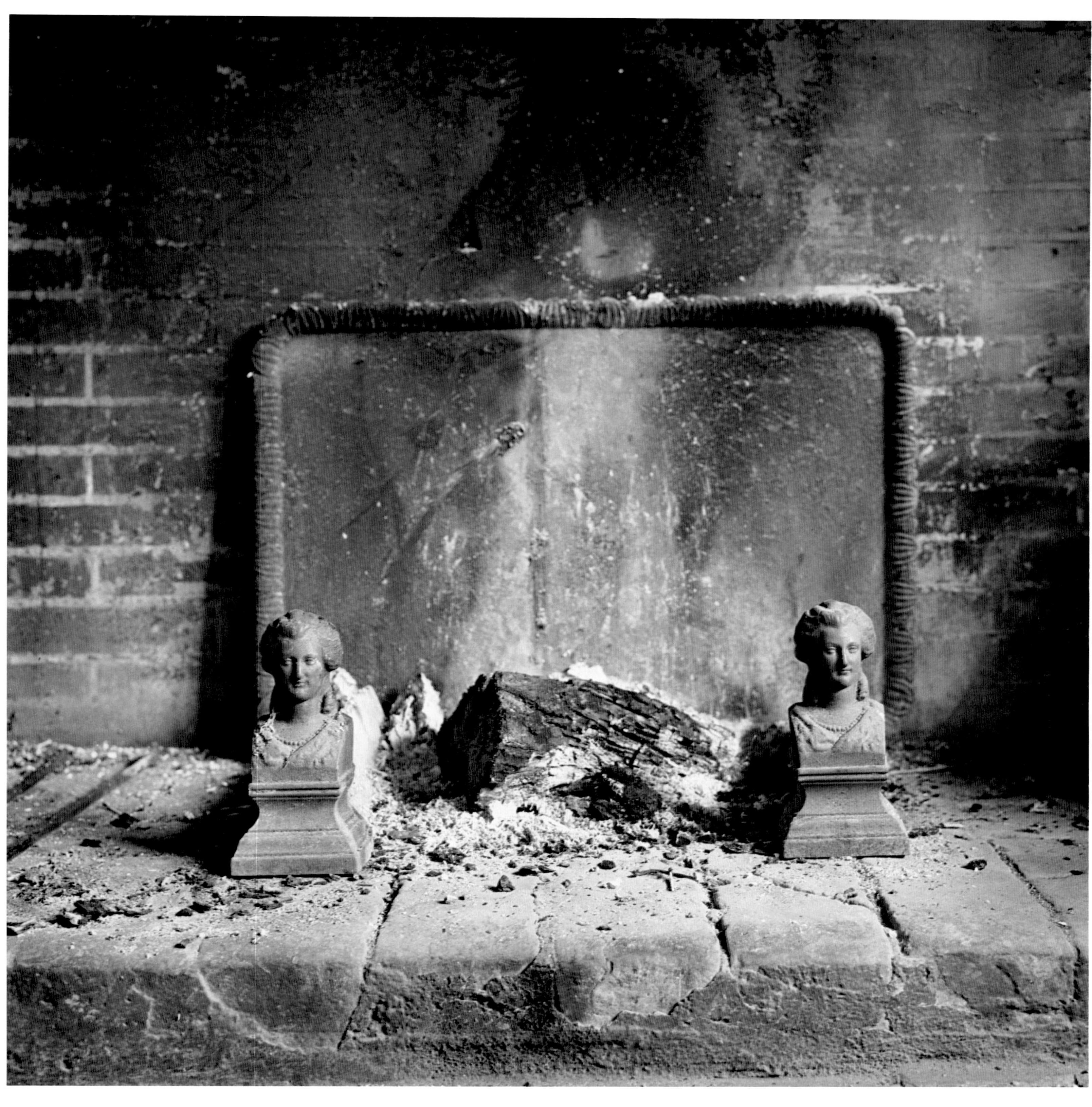

Fireplace II, Bourgogne. 1980

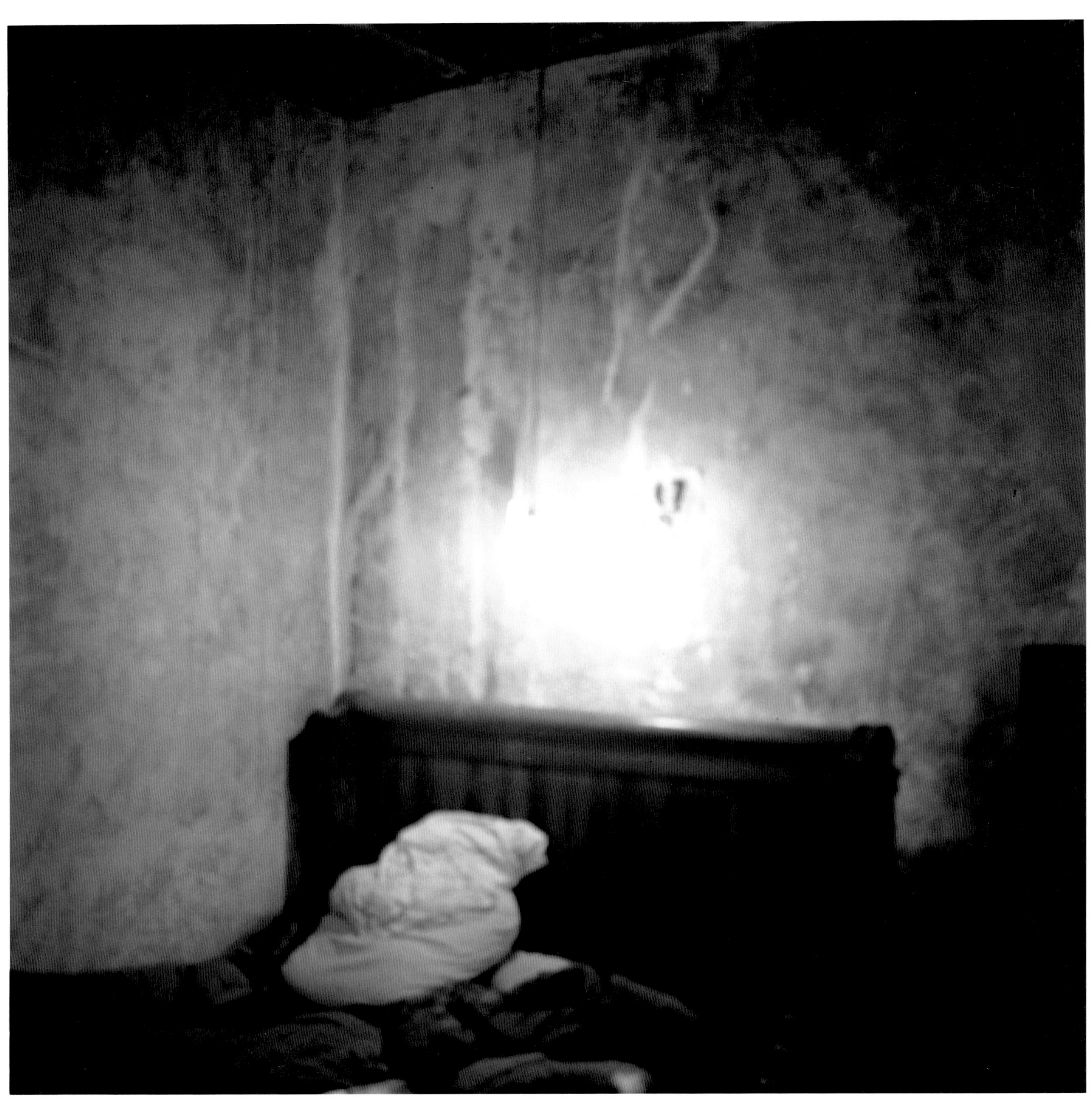

Pillow, Bed, Wall, Bourgogne. 1980

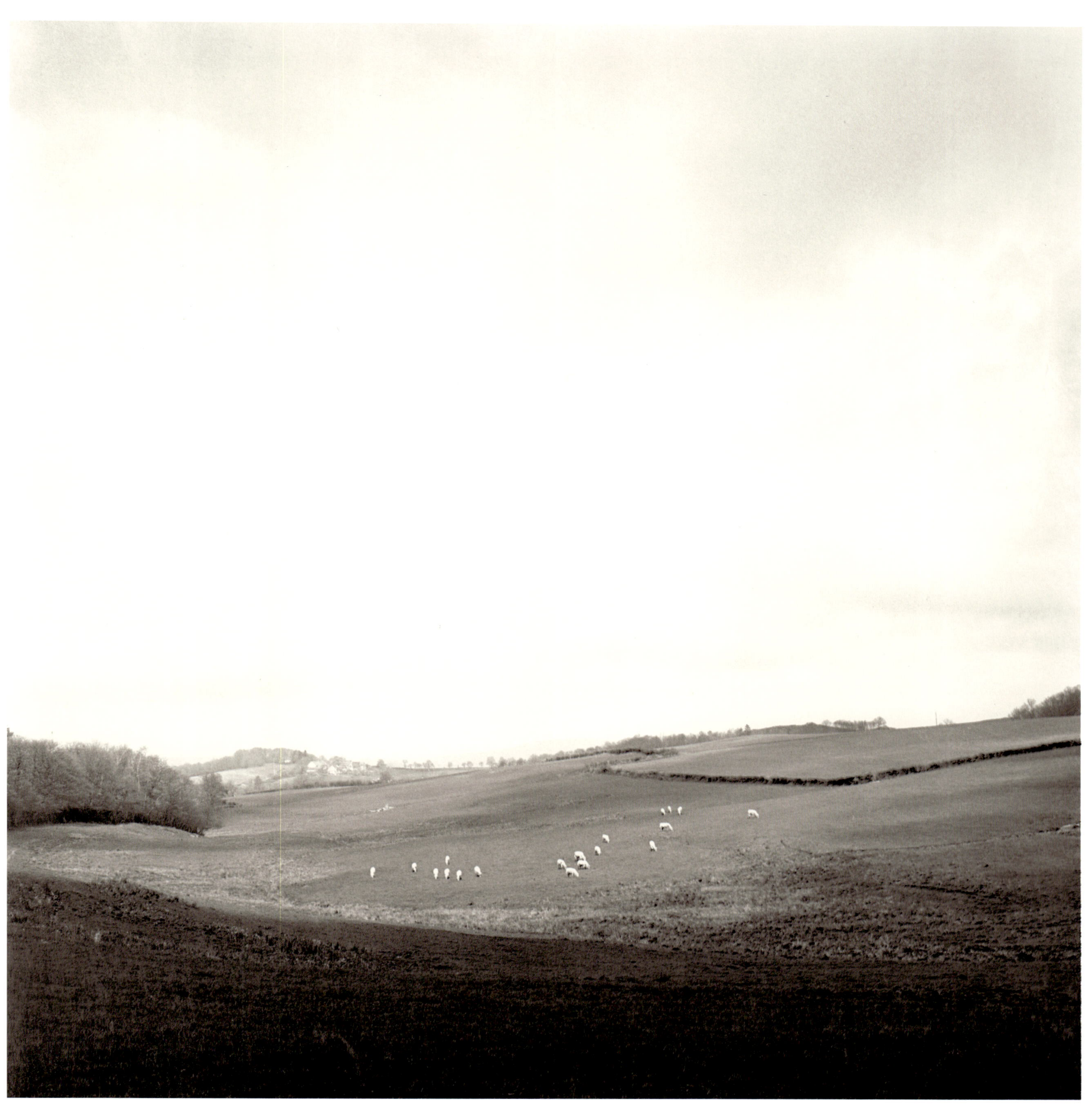

Cows, Bourgogne. 1980

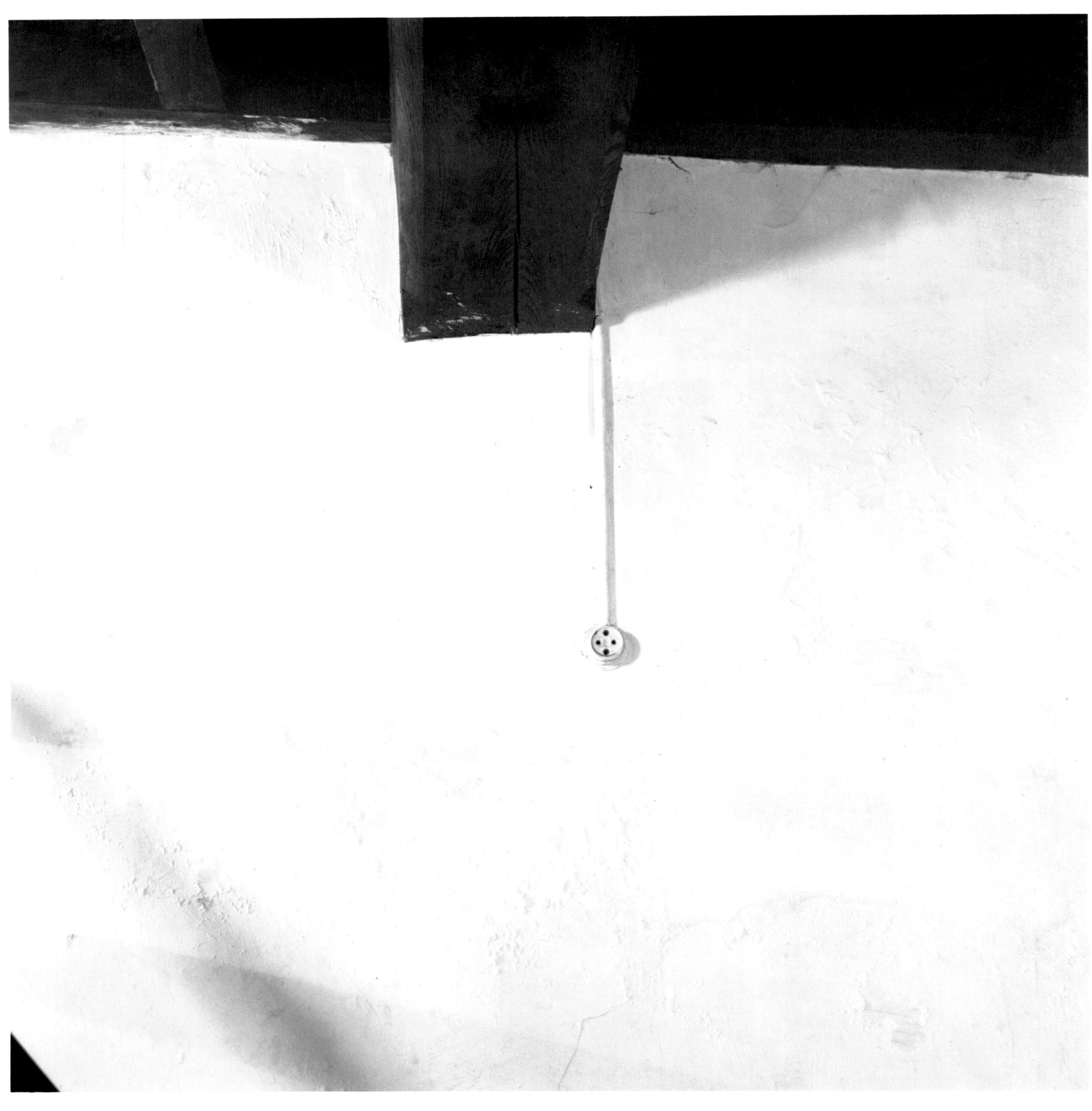

Electric Socket, Bourgogne. 1980

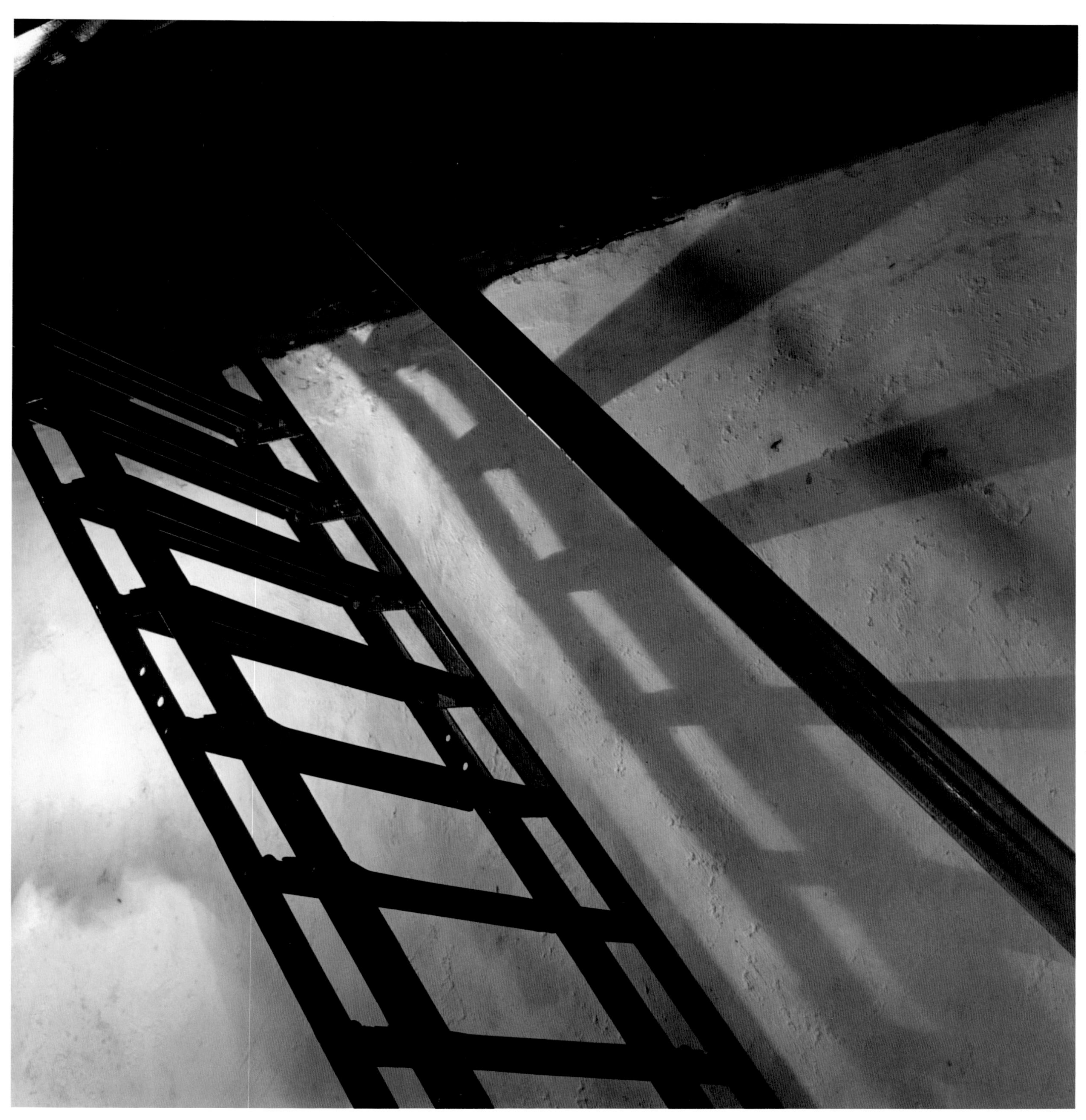

Stairs, Bourgogne. 1980

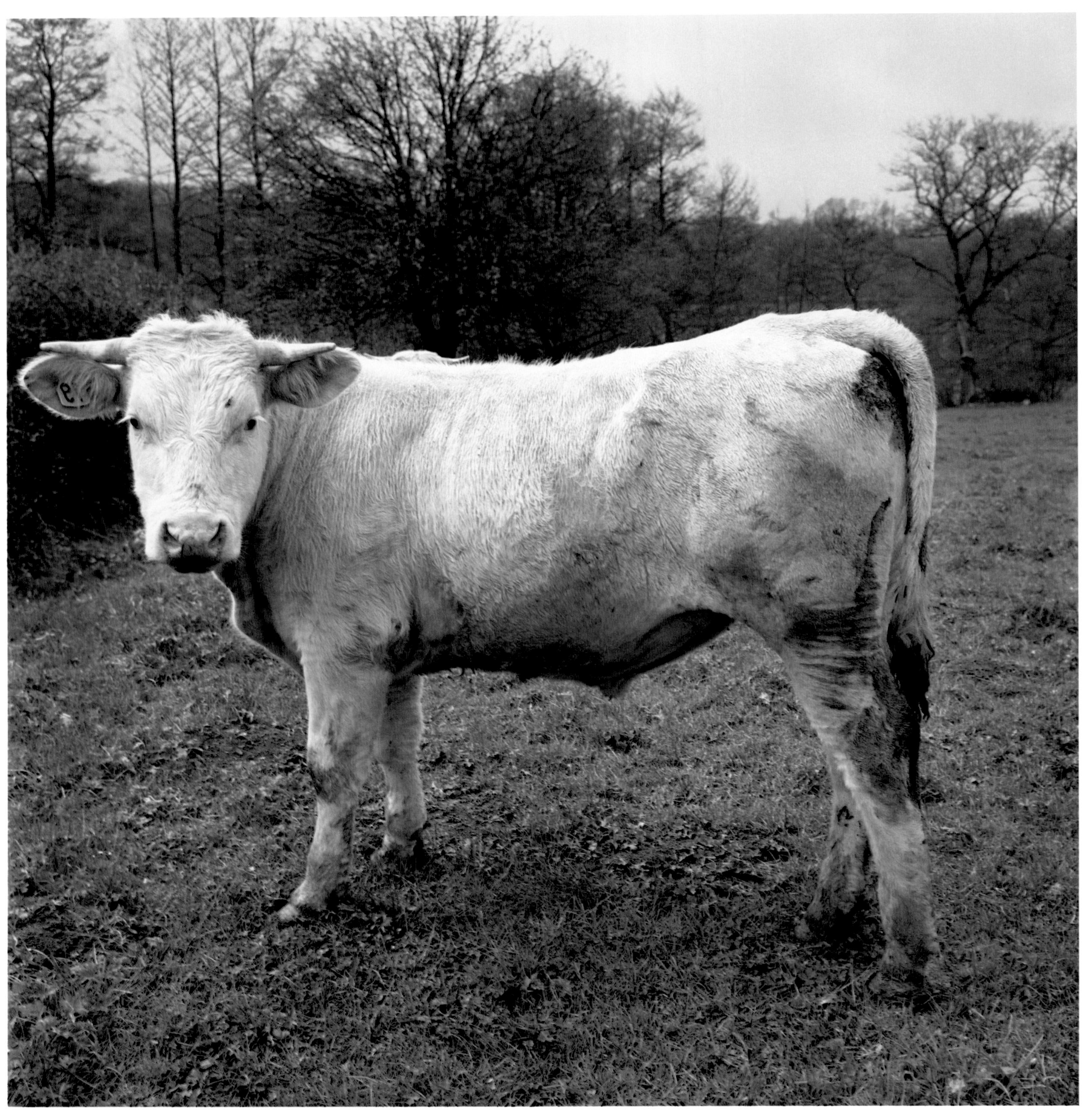

Ox, Bourgogne. 1980

Works

1980-1987

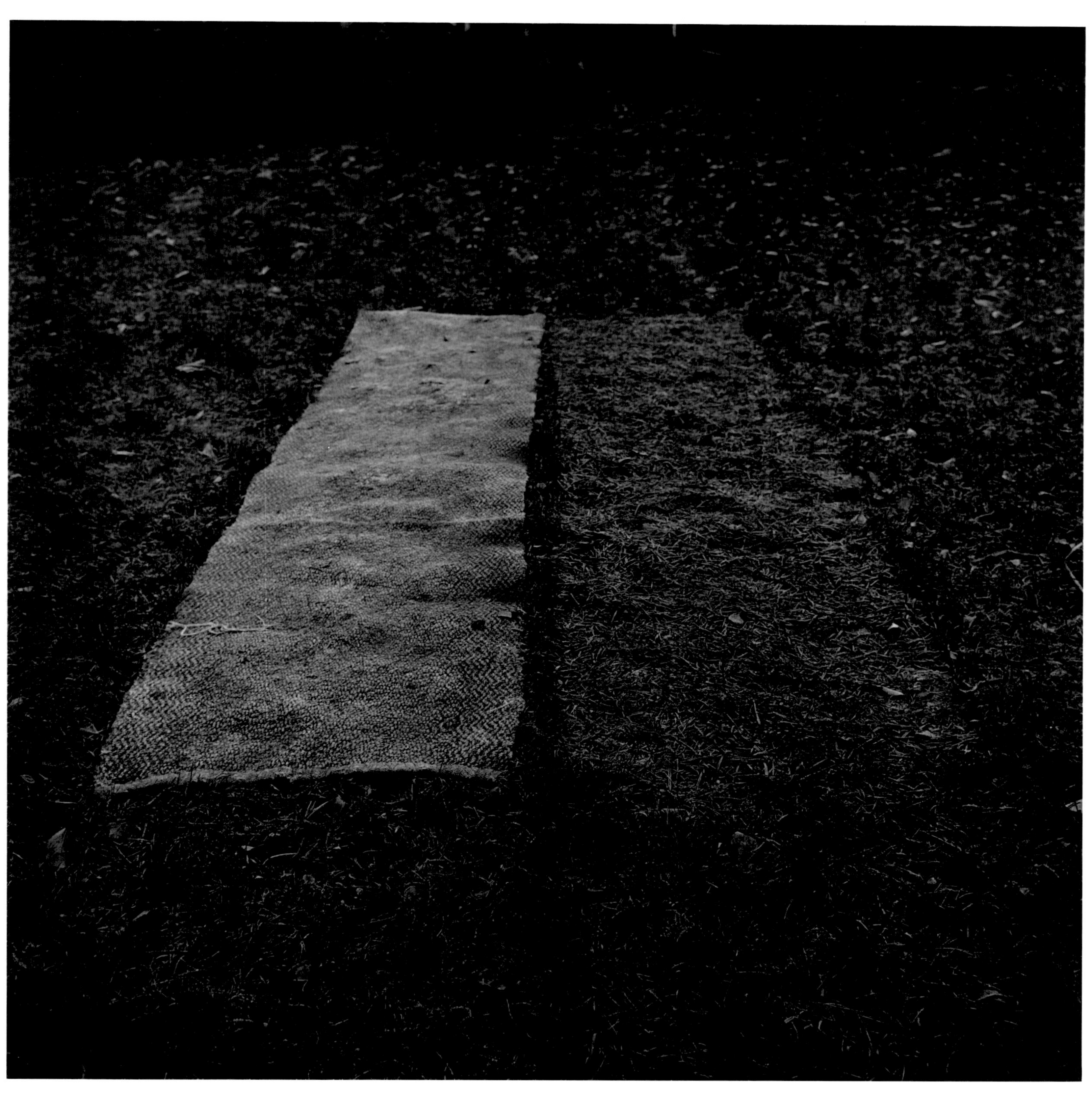

Turned-over. 1981

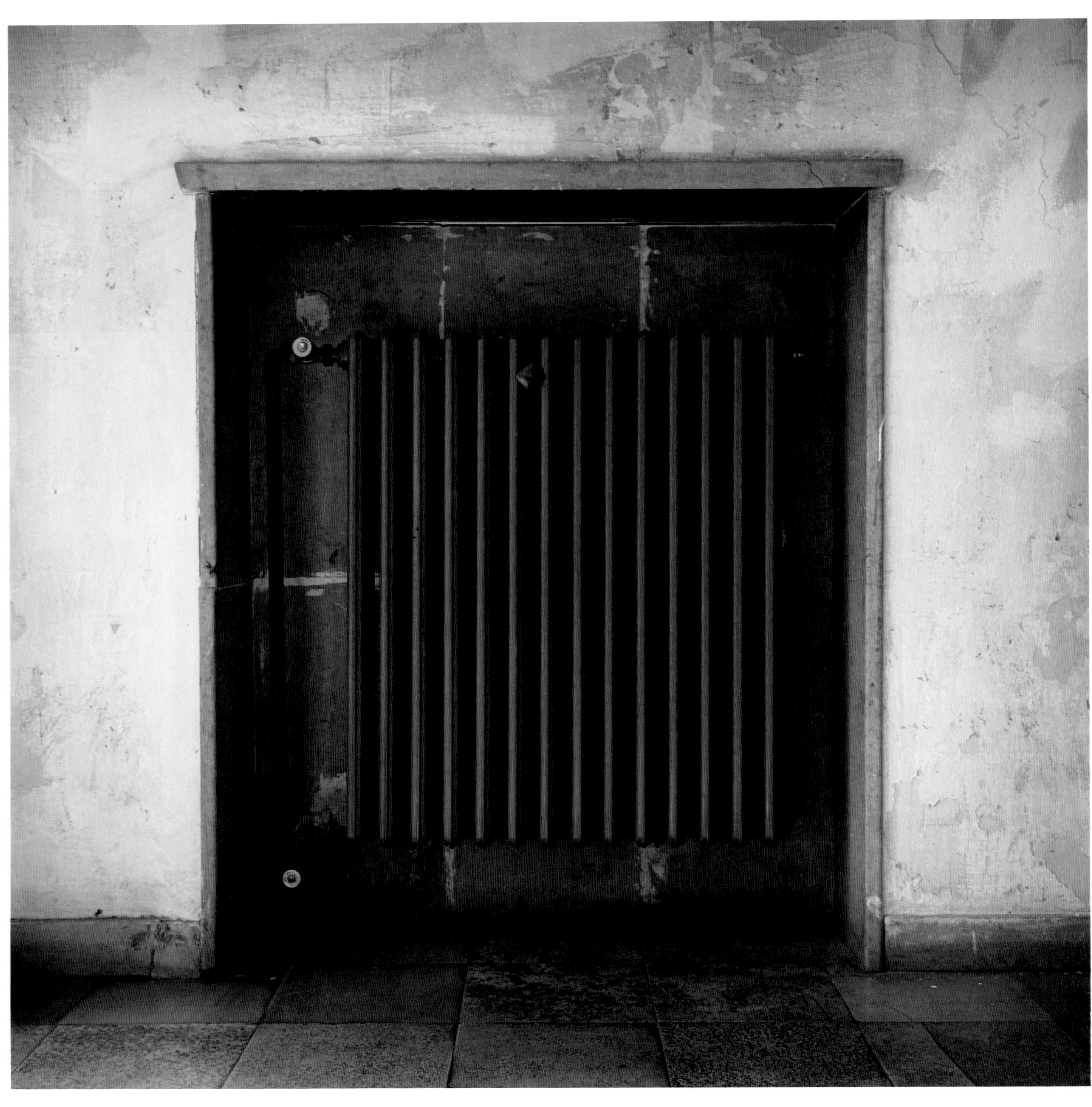

Radiator, Düsseldorf. 1982

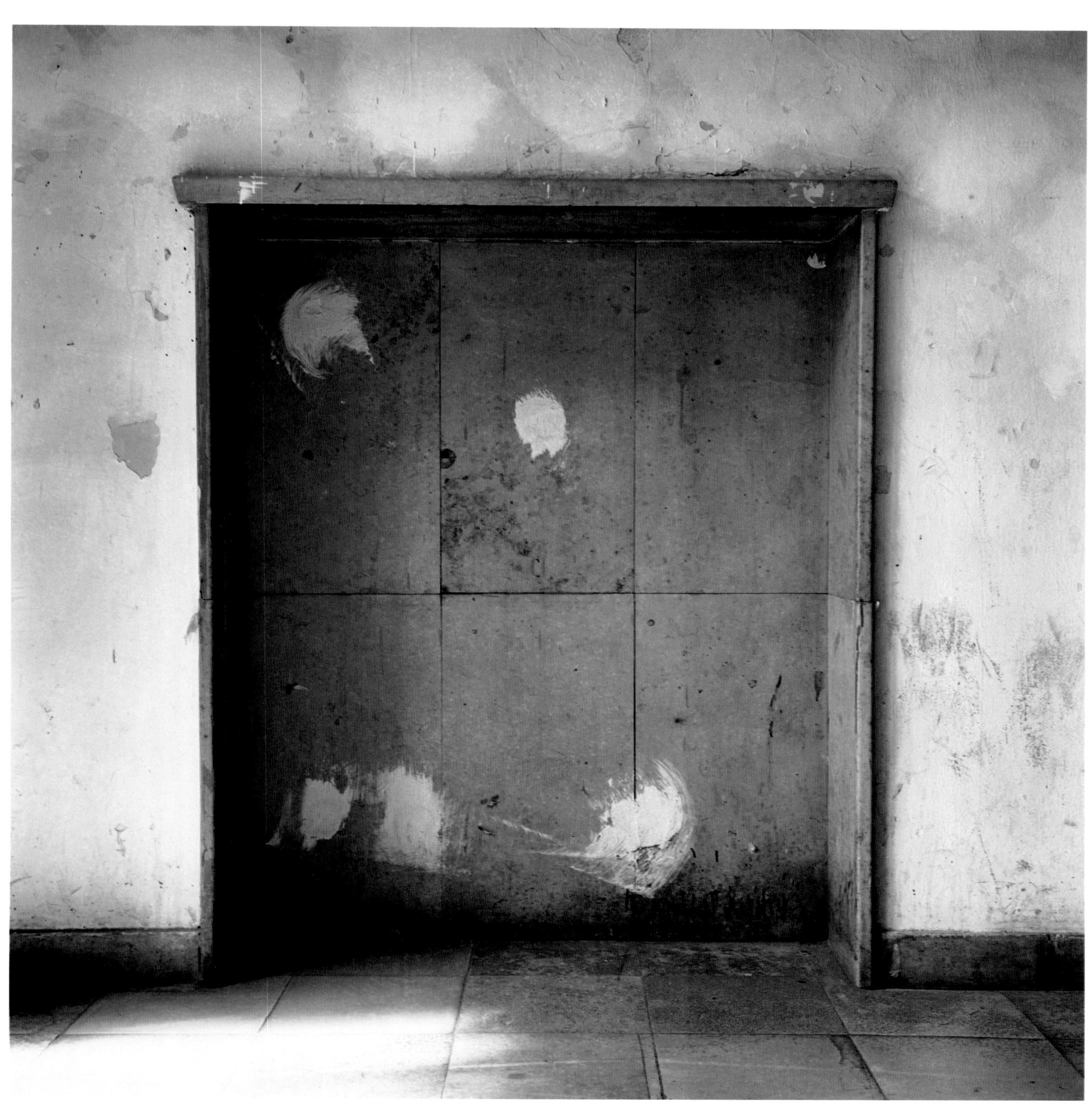

Radiator Gone, Düsseldorf. 1982

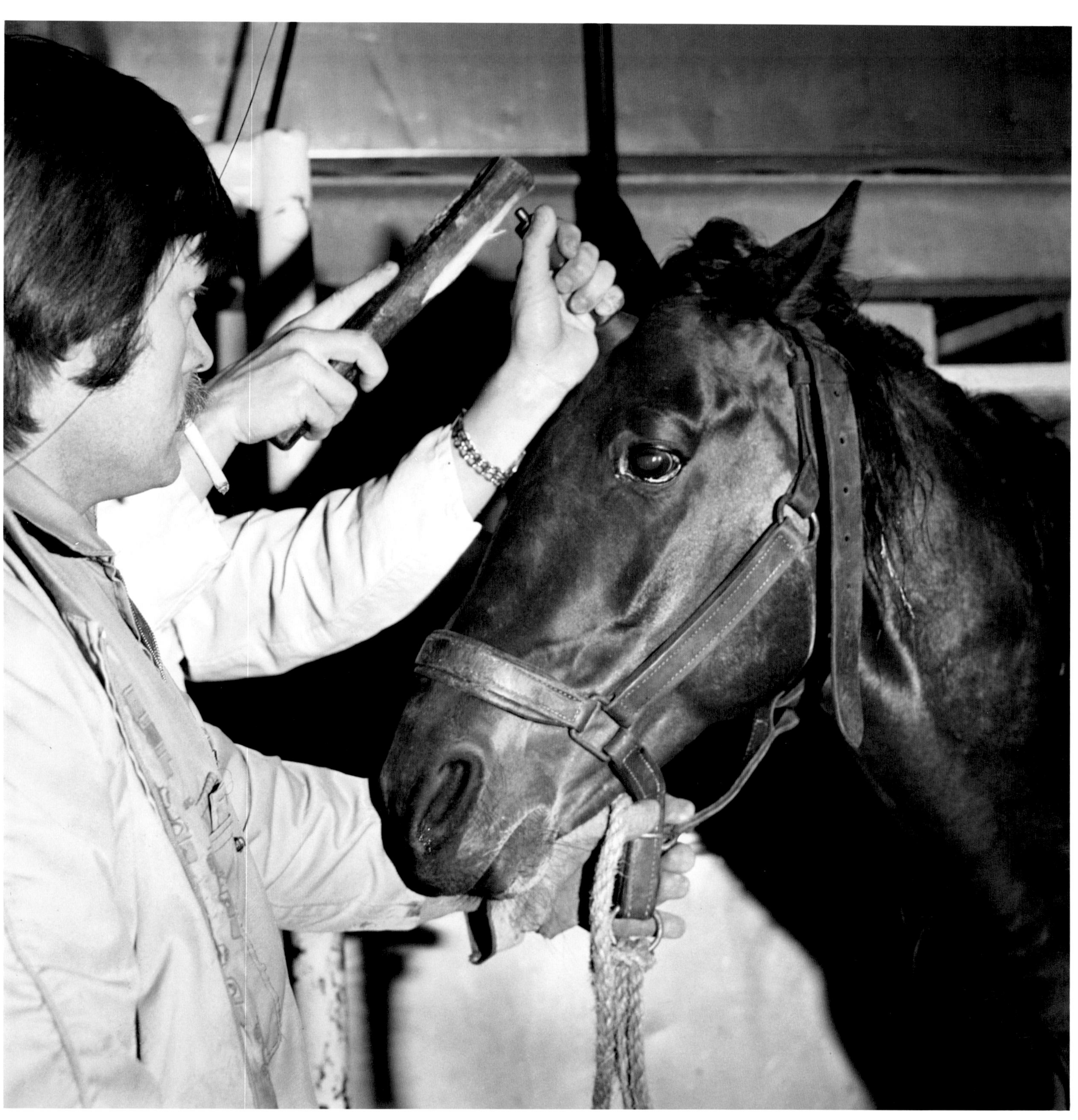

The Death of a Horse, Jessheim. 1984

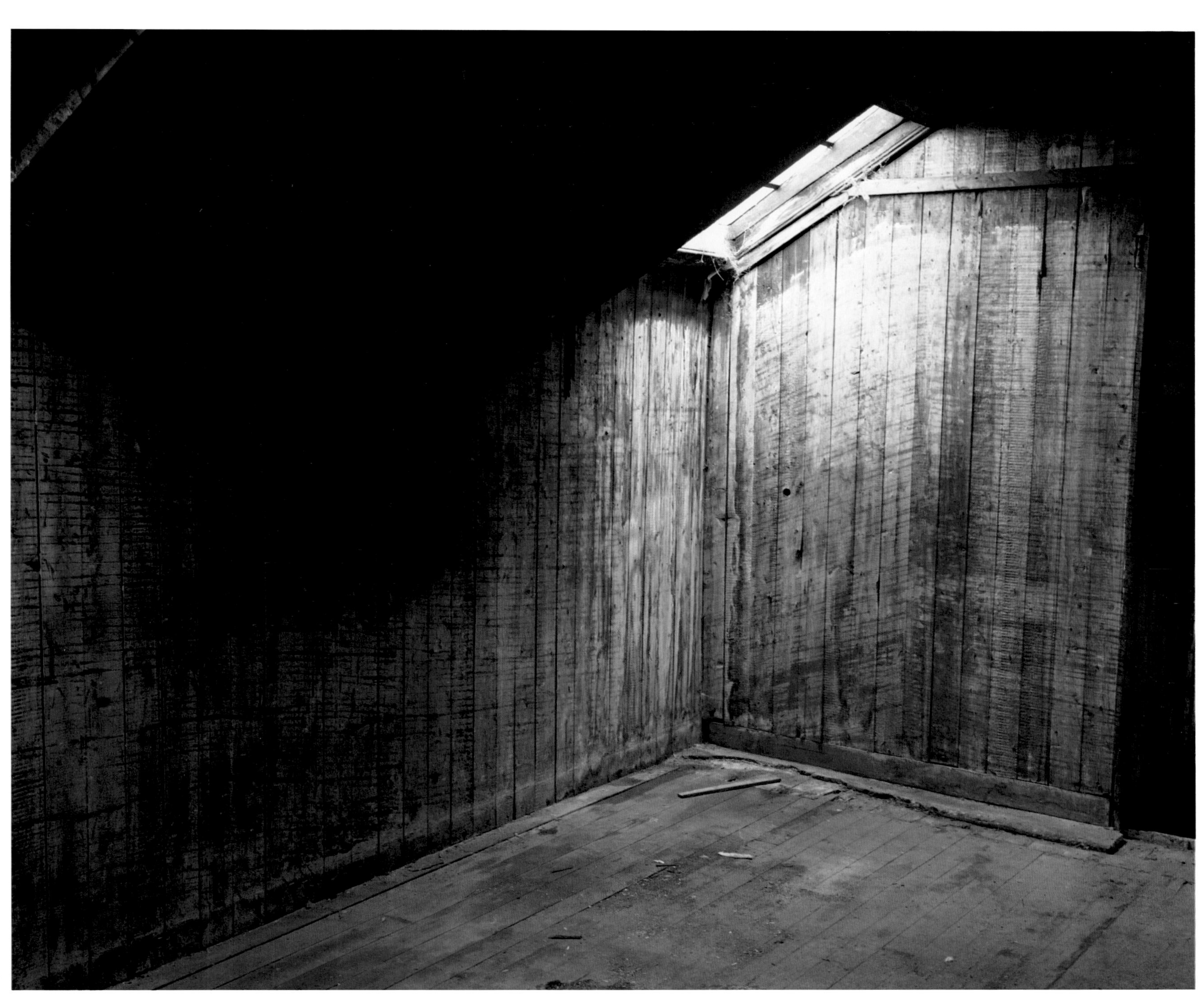

Attic, United Sardines Factory, Bergen. 1984

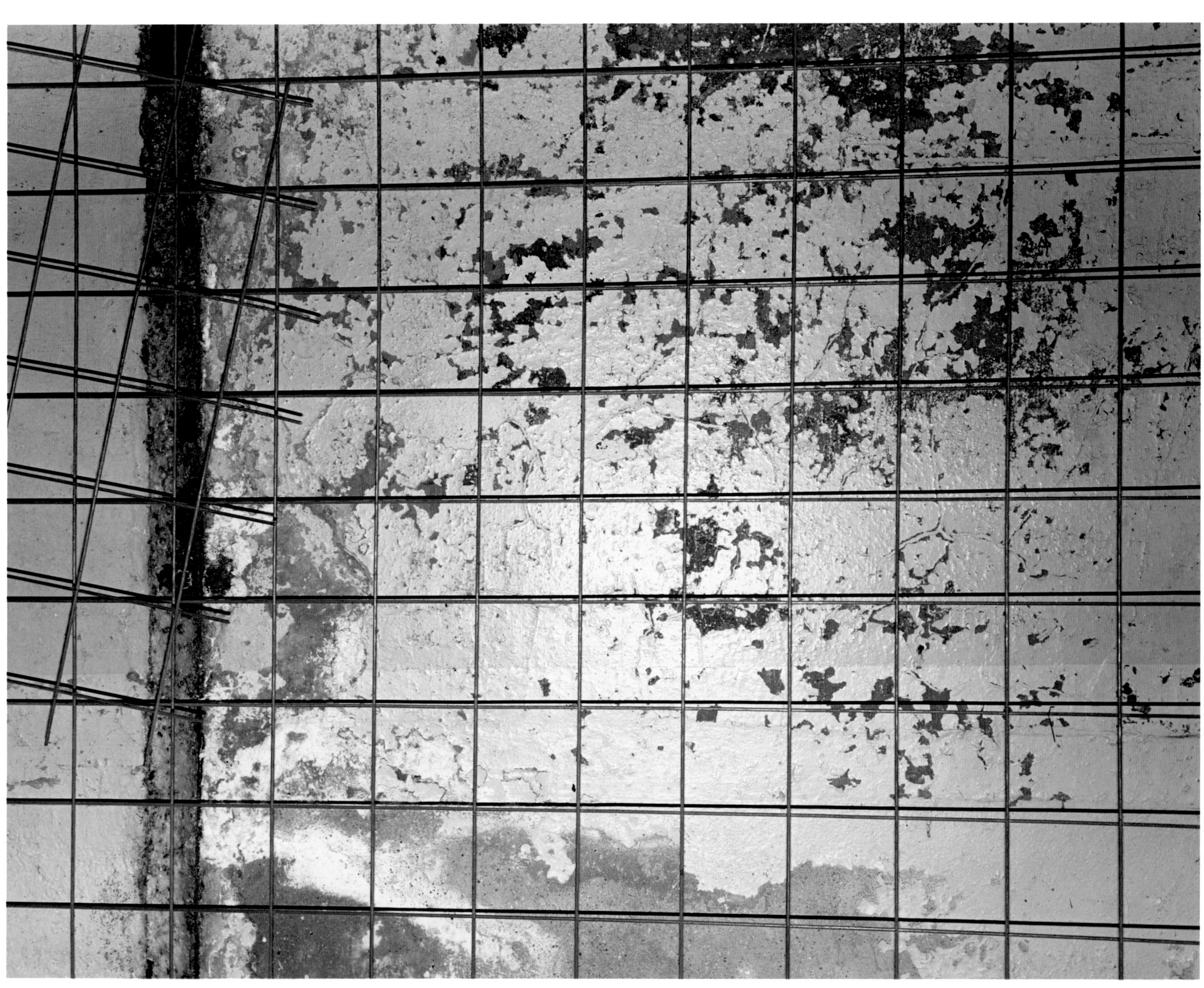

Grid, United Sardines Factory, Bergen. 1984

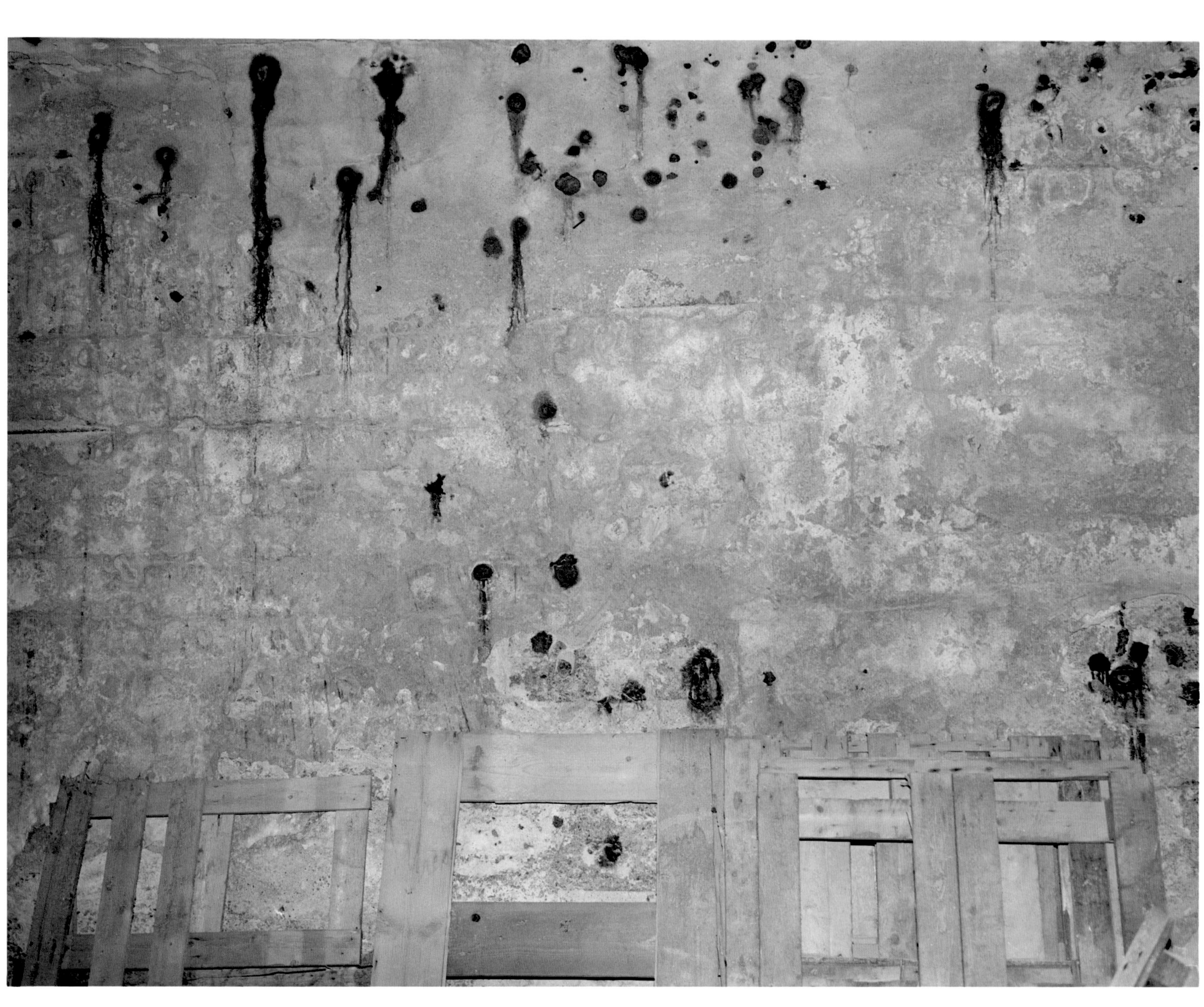

Wall, United Sardines Factory, Bergen. 1984

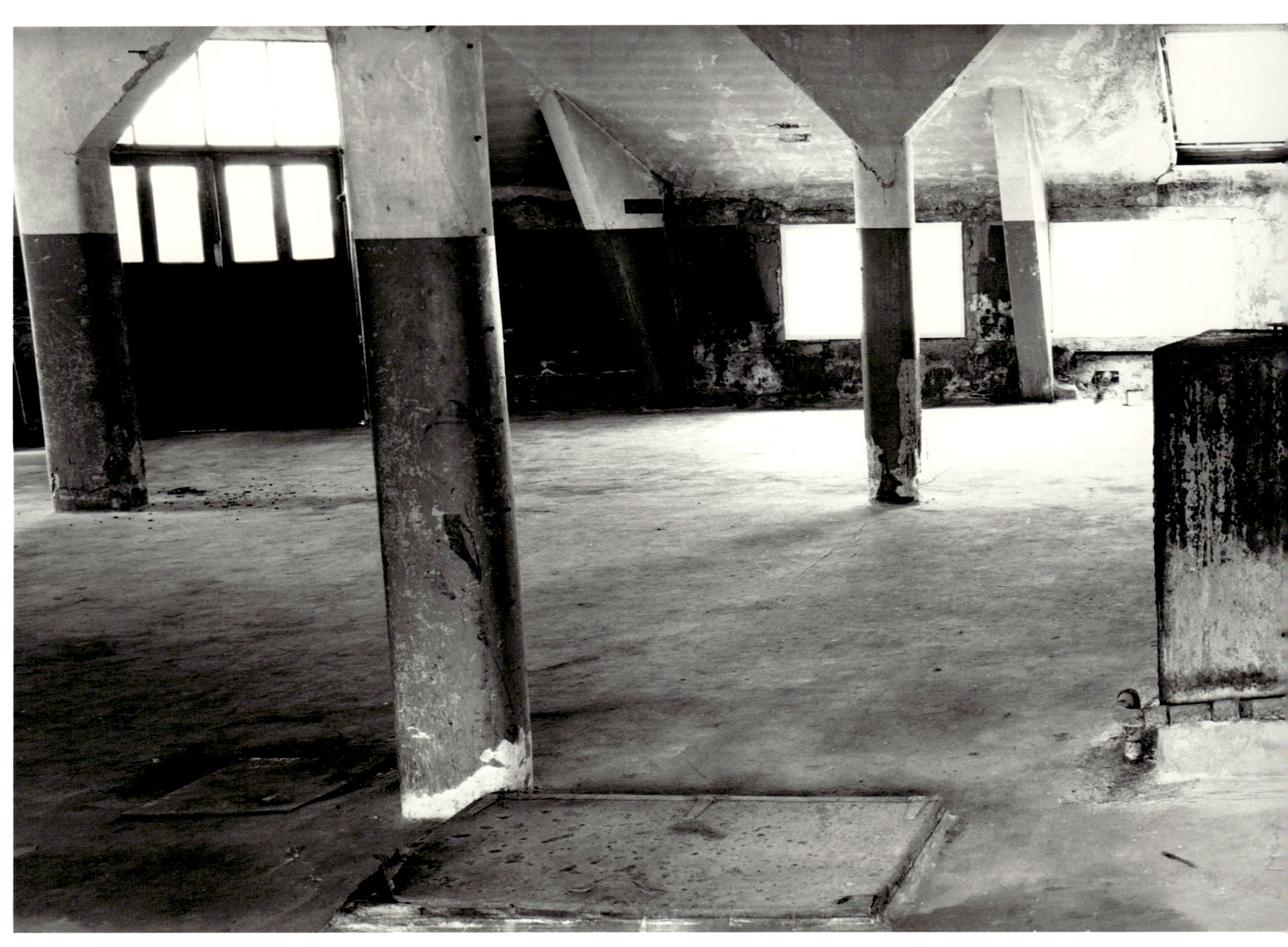

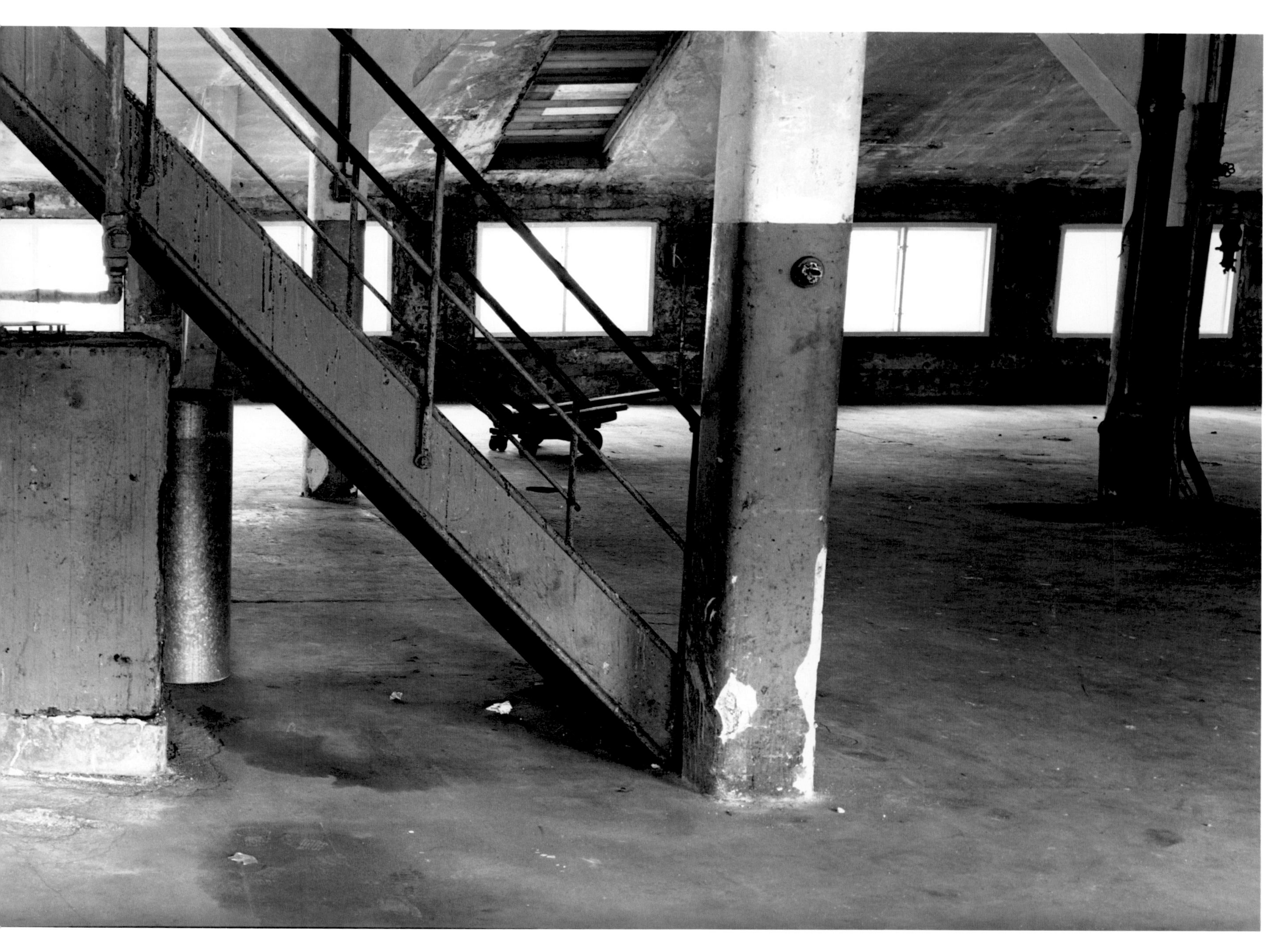

Production Hall, United Sardines Factory, Bergen. 1984

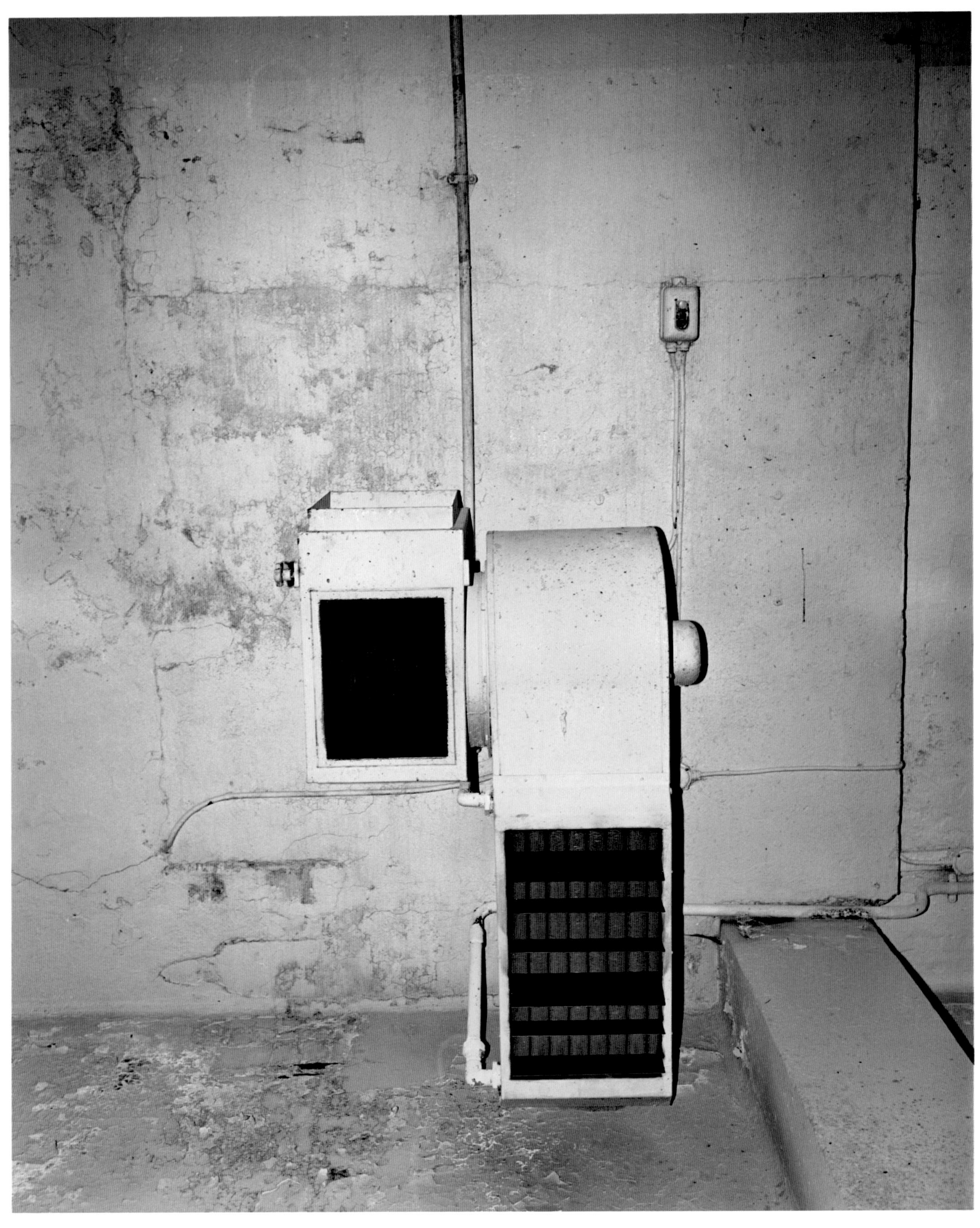

Ventilator, United Sardines Factory, Bergen. 1984

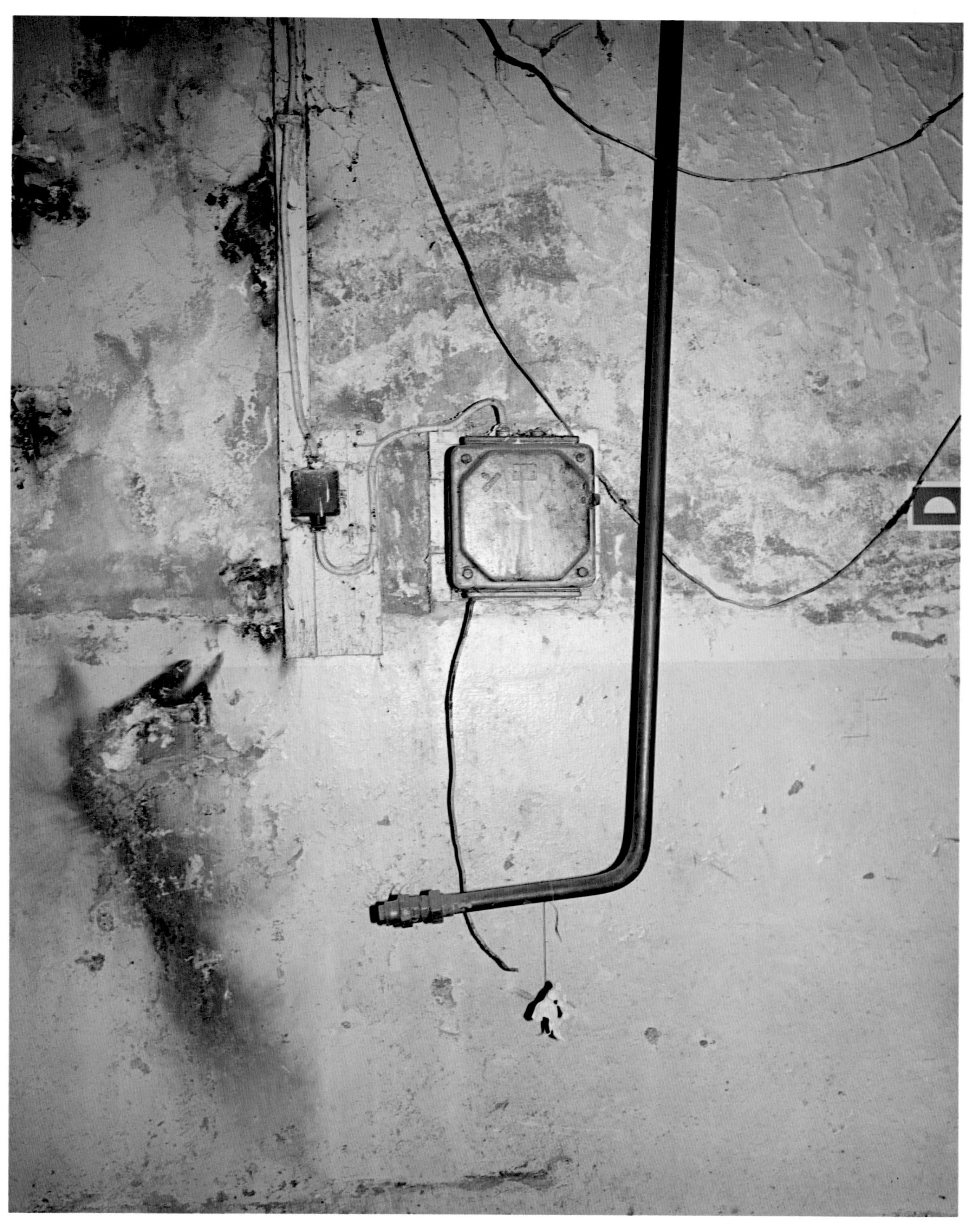

Electrical Socket, Tube and Balloon, United Sardines Factory, Bergen. 1984

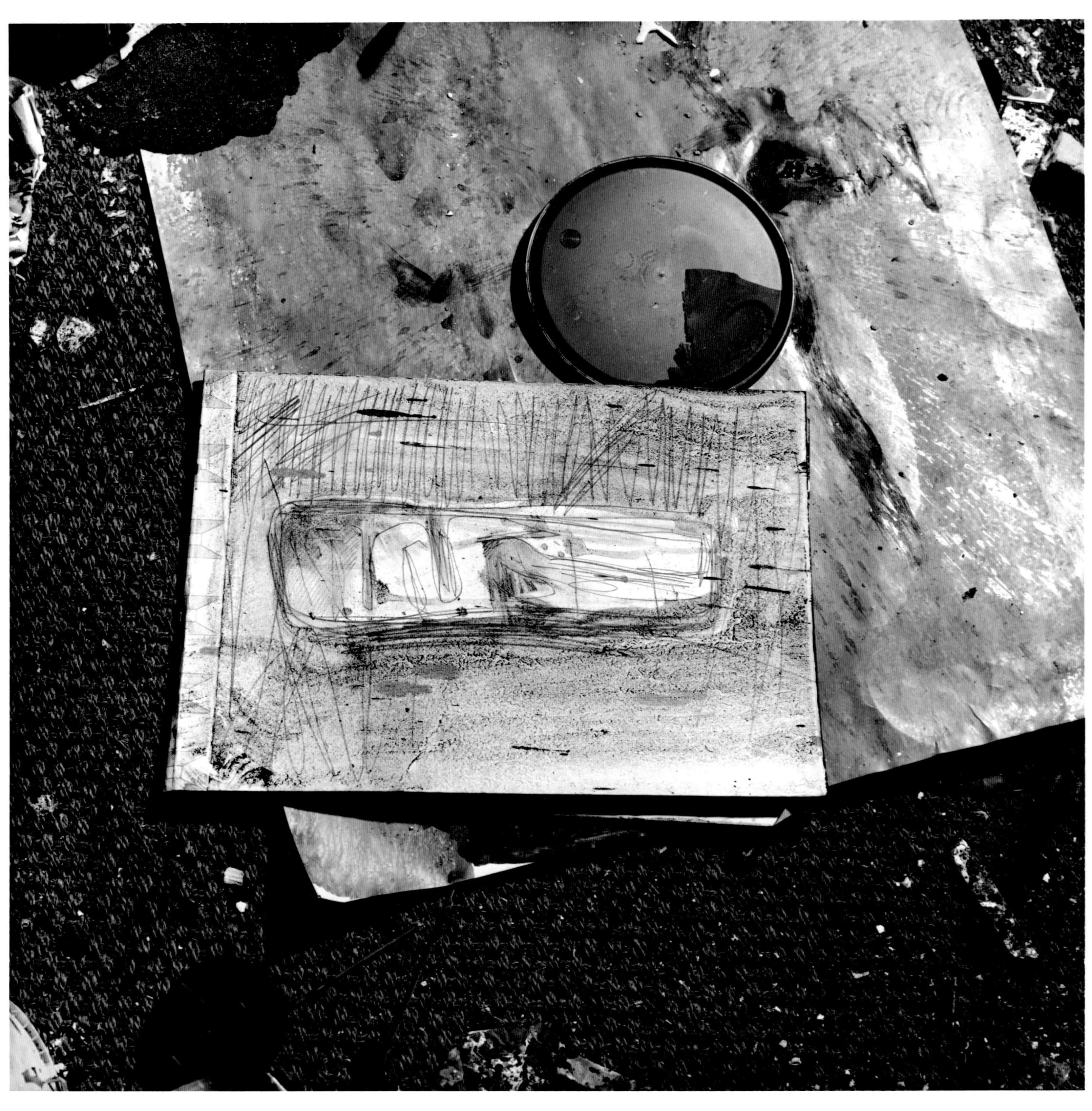

A Drawing, Kristian's Room. 1985

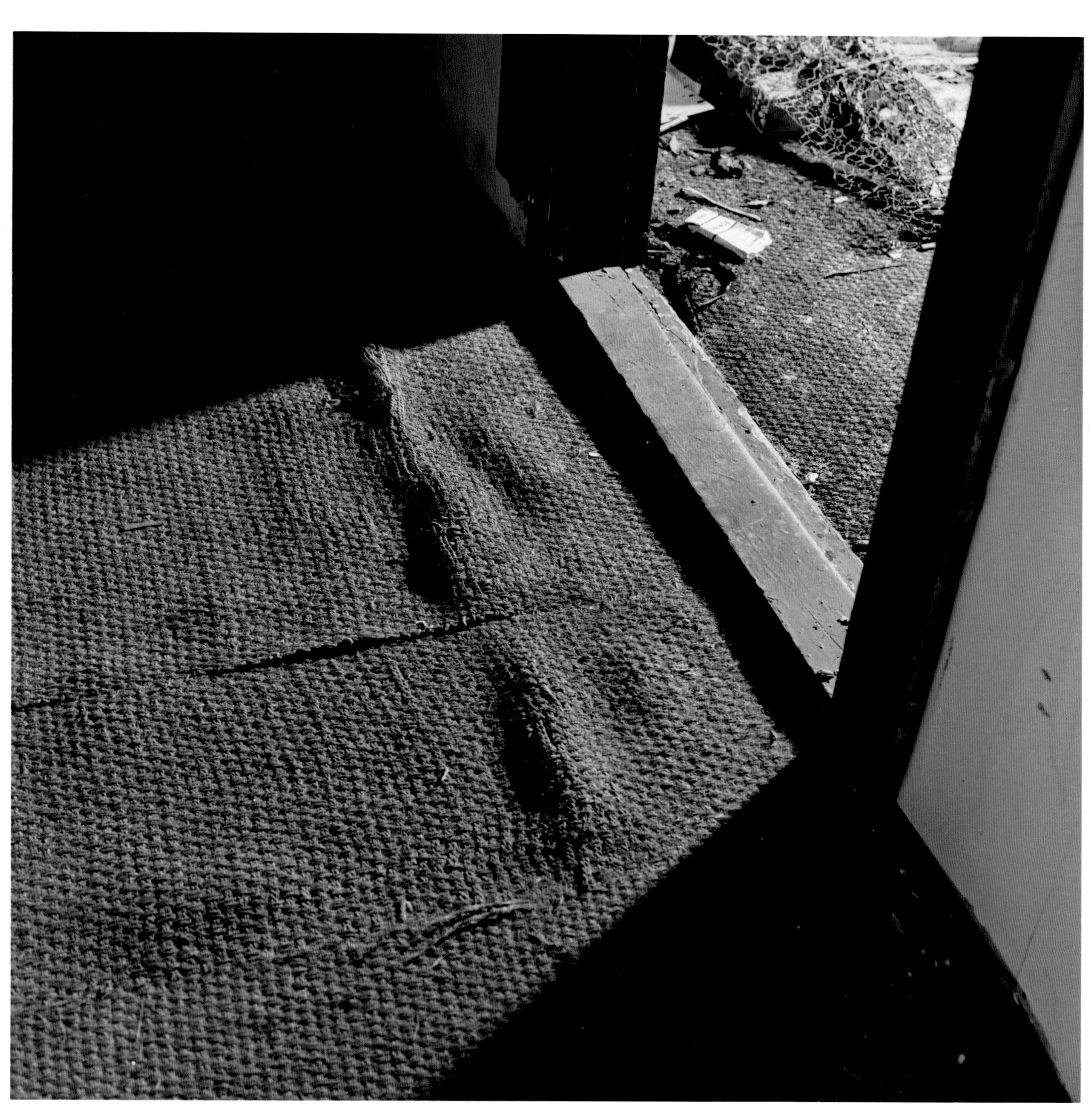

The Doorway, Kristian's Room. 1985

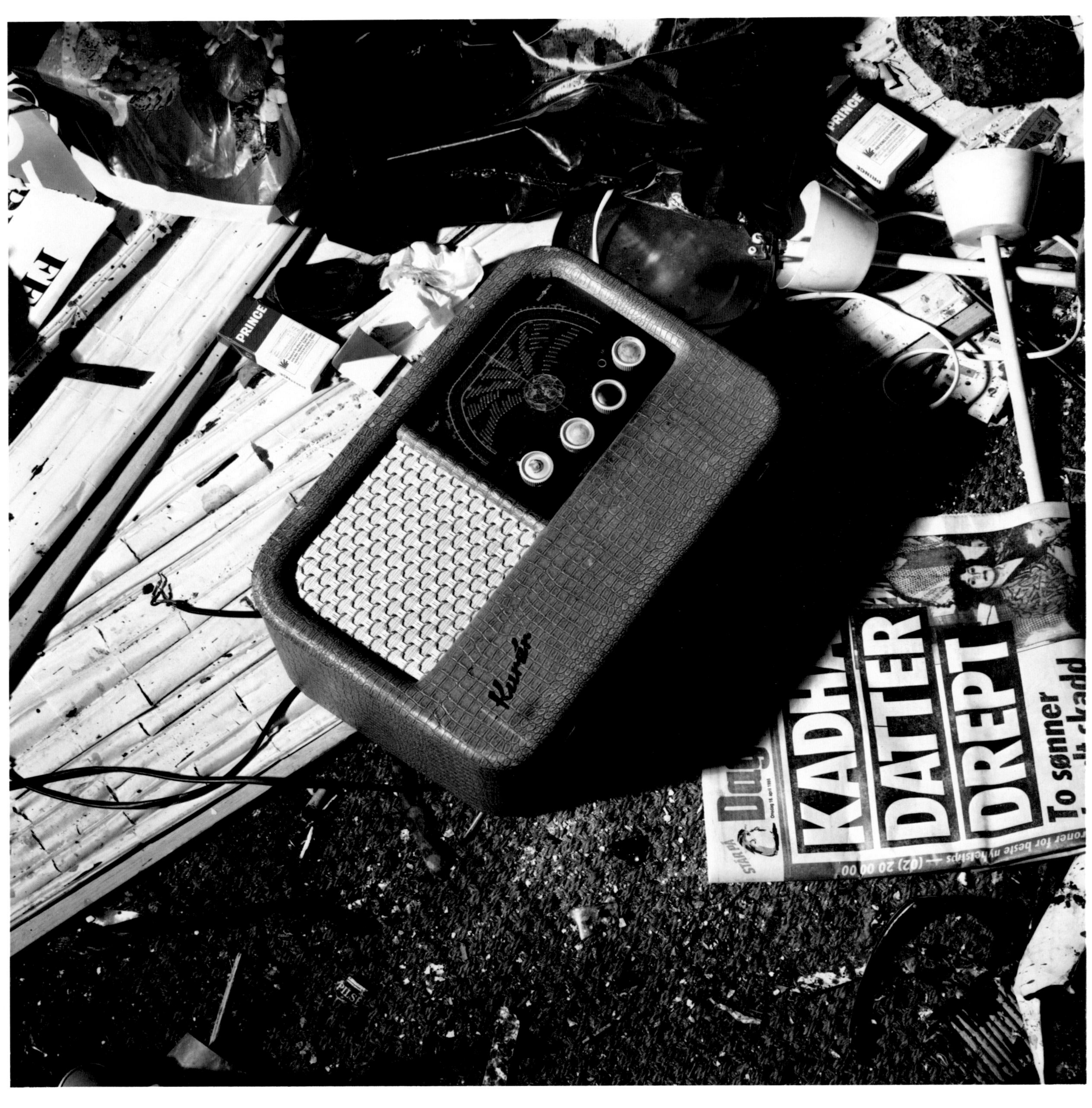

The Radio, Kristian's Room. 1985

Asylum

1979-1982

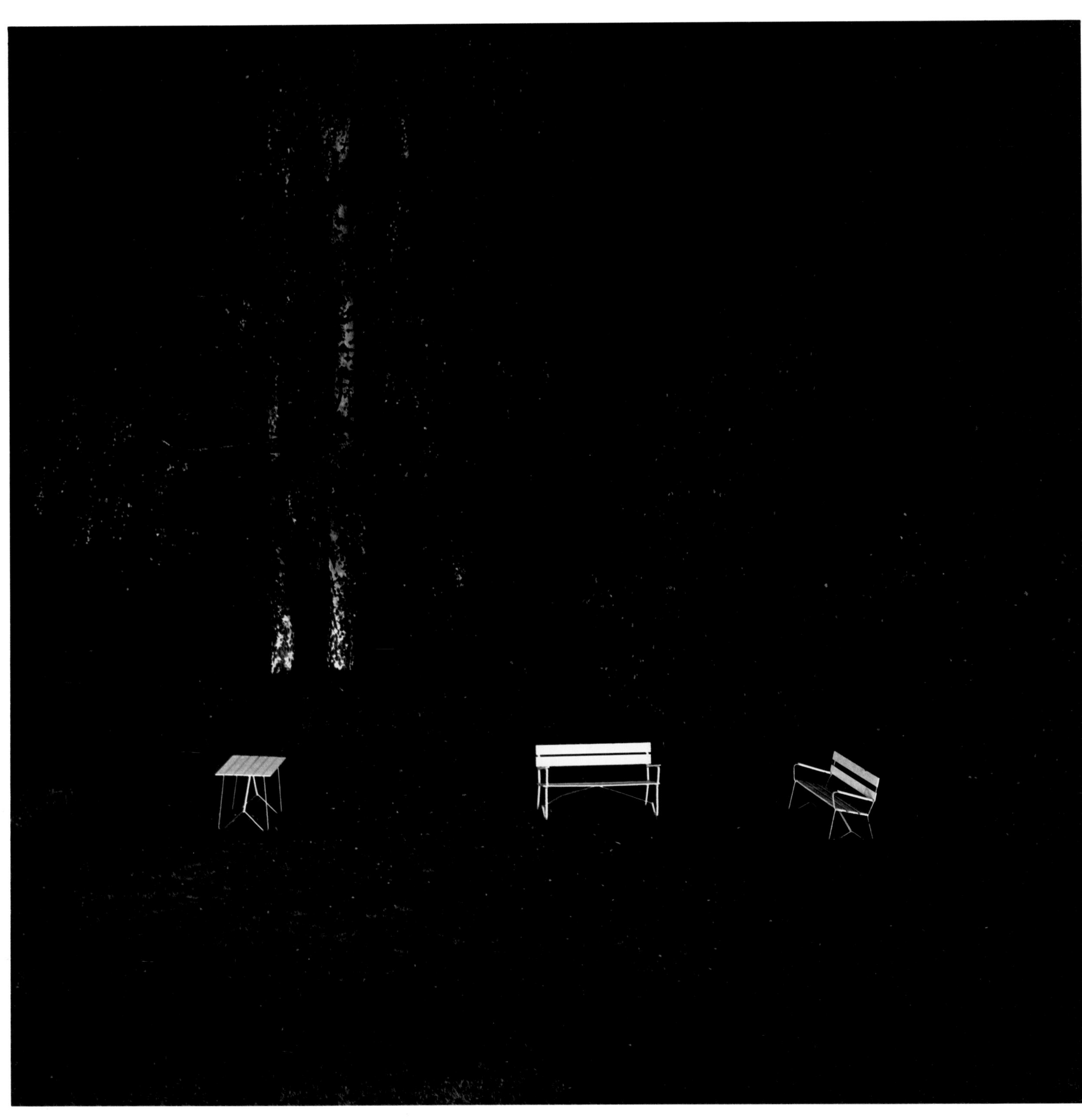

Two Benches and a Table. 1981

Asylum

Mental hospitals are frightening places where people have crossed a threshold. It is necessary for us on the outside to imagine them as benign places and to blindly hope they are beneficial to those who live there. They are, for most of us, in that category of things we do not think about.

In the series of photographs made between 1979 and 1982, Dag Alveng has frontally attacked the secrets of the psychiatric institution. His clear depiction of its pertinent details—walls, furniture, and ephemera—reveals the possibilities of existential fact. We believe we are seeing the objects themselves and not their representation in photographs. What is depicted becomes symbolic of passivity, boredom, repetition, violence, intimidation, and routine. Such a revelation is more challenging than mere transformation, since as viewers, we are forced to respond to descriptions seemingly unfiltered by the photographer.

Alveng, who made these photographs while working as the institution's nightwatchman, takes us on a surreptitious journey through its corridors and rooms, revealing to us harrowing and sorrowful truths.

Susan Kismaric

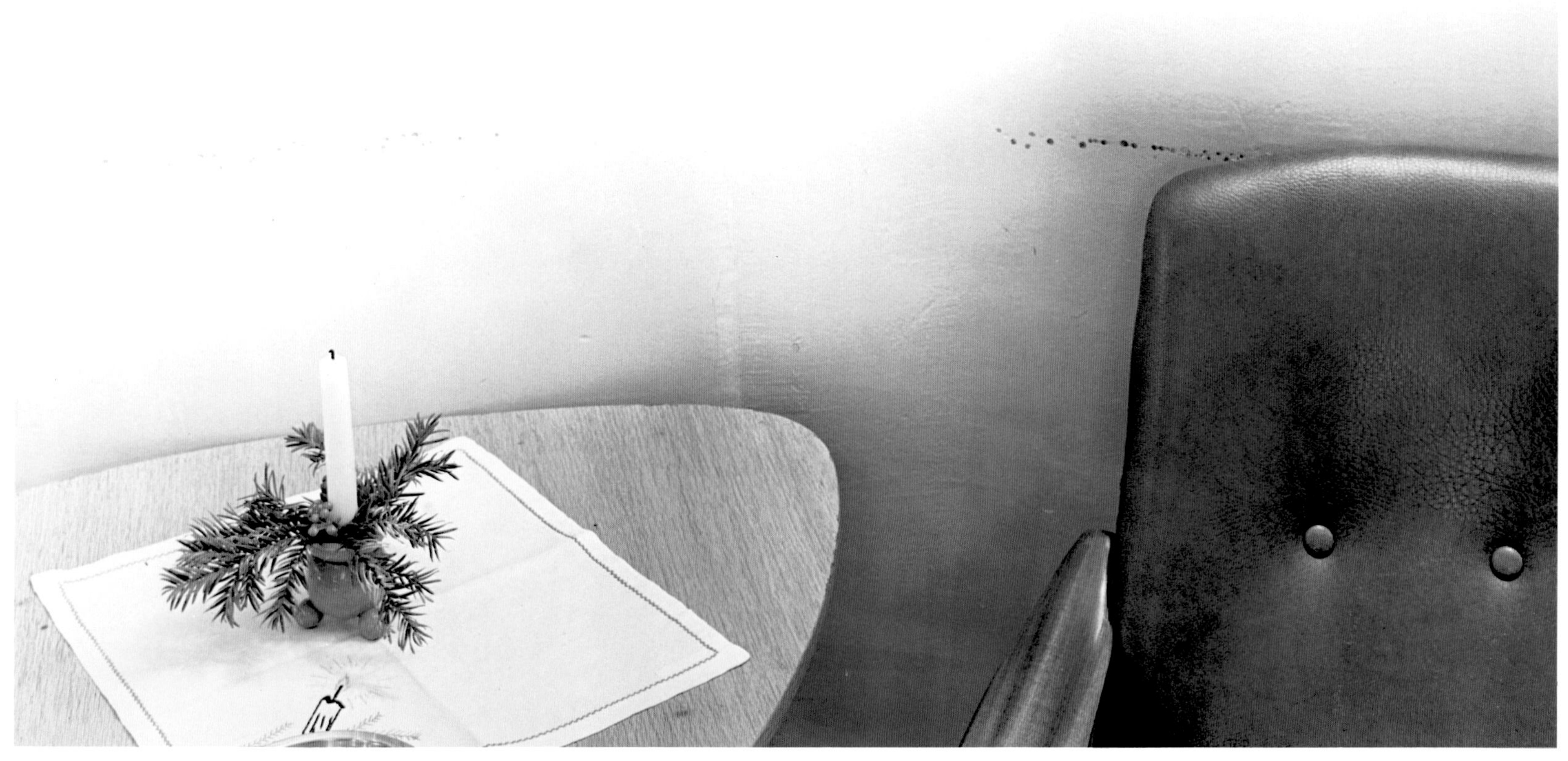

Wall with Marks from Chair, Christmas. 1982

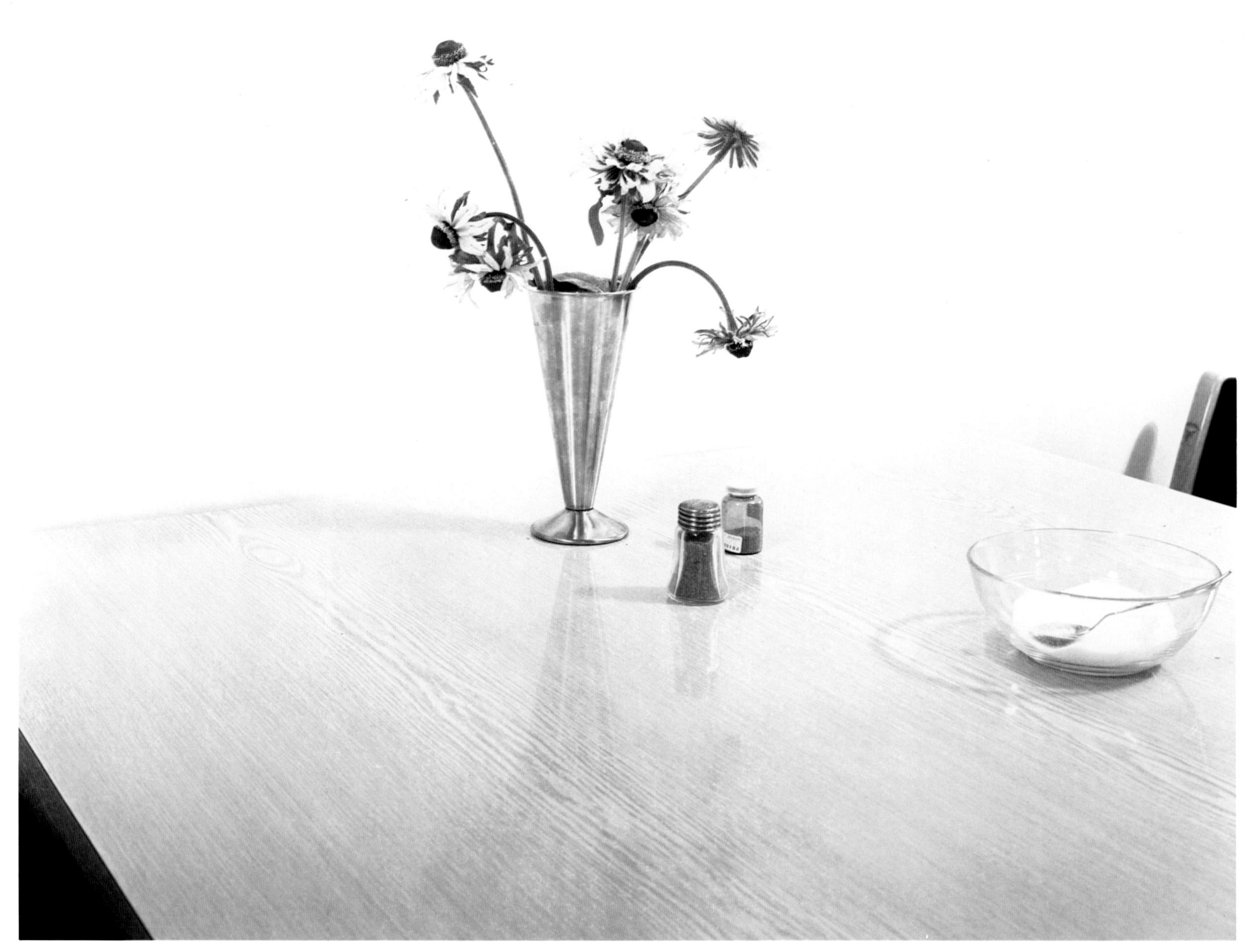

Flowers. 1981

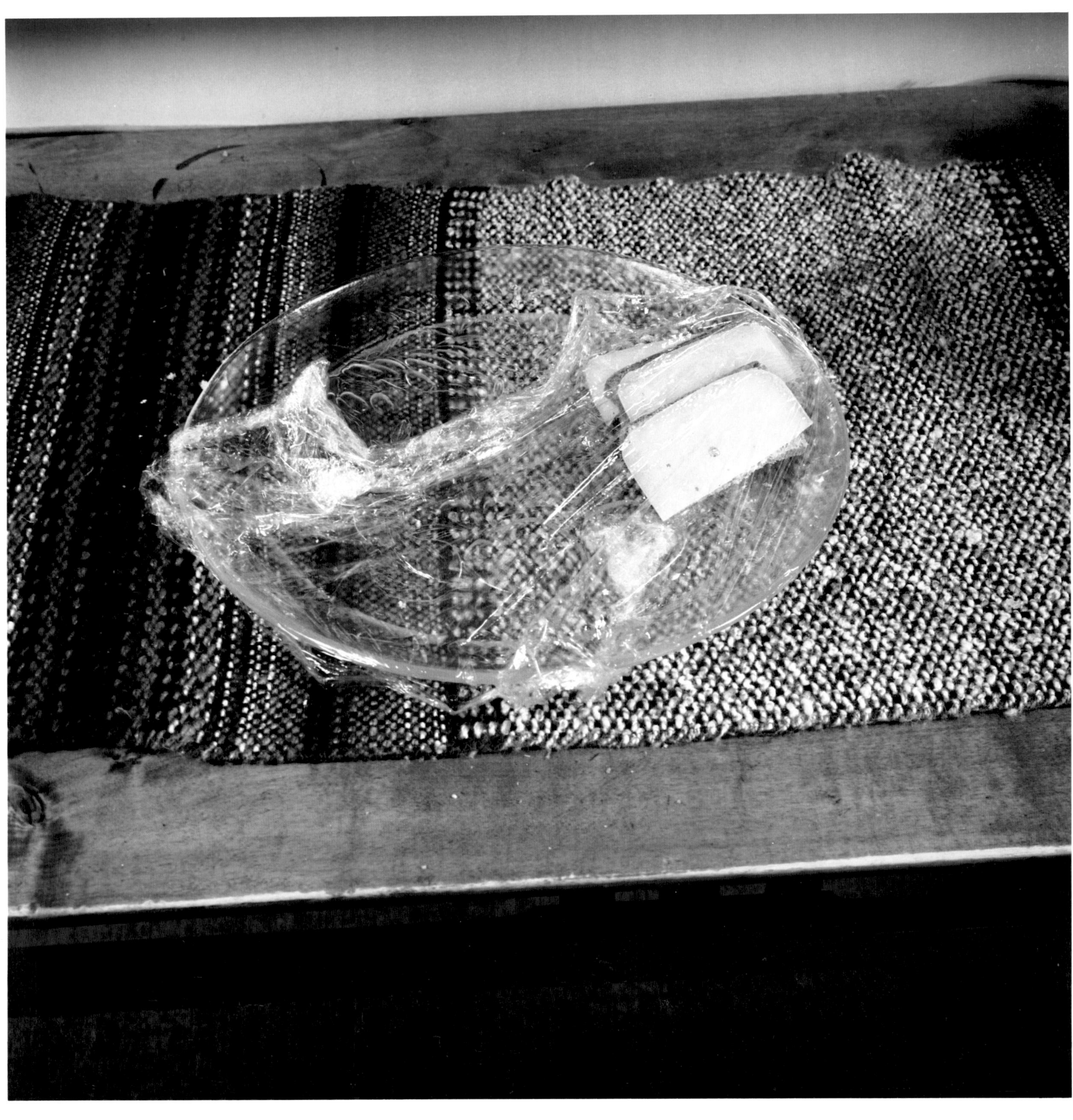

Food in Plastic. 1979

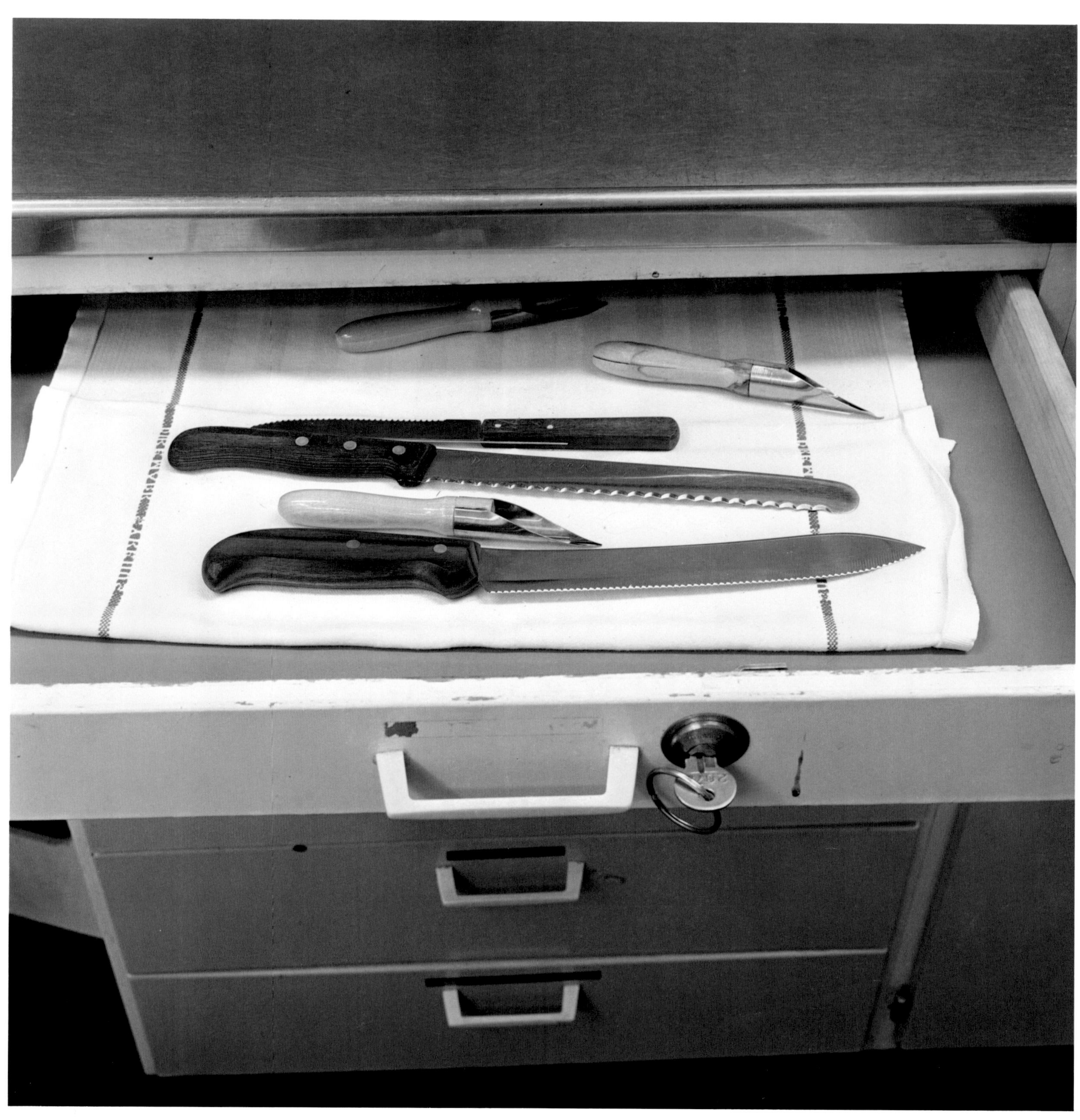

Lock and Knives. 1979

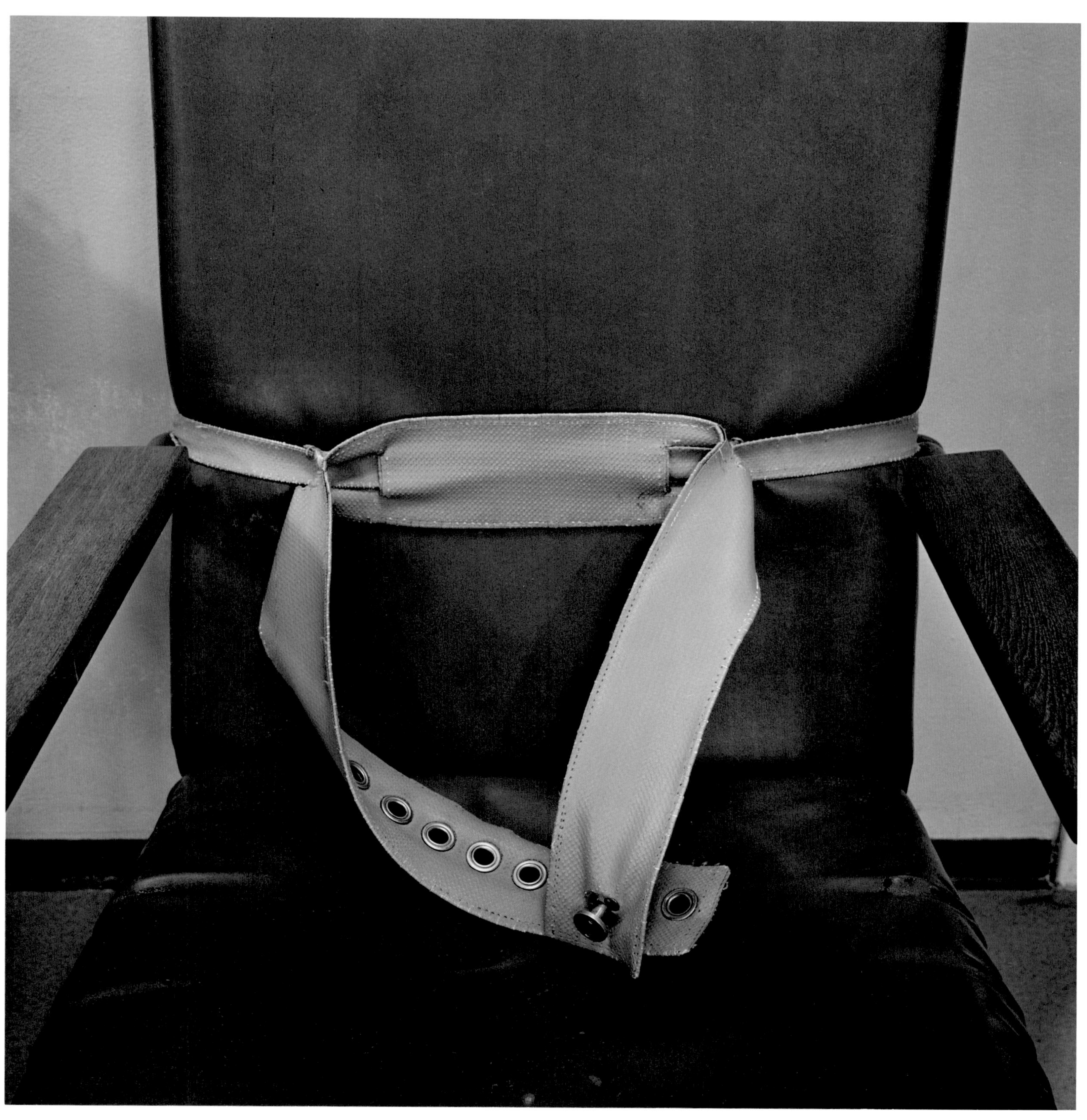

Strap Chair. 1980

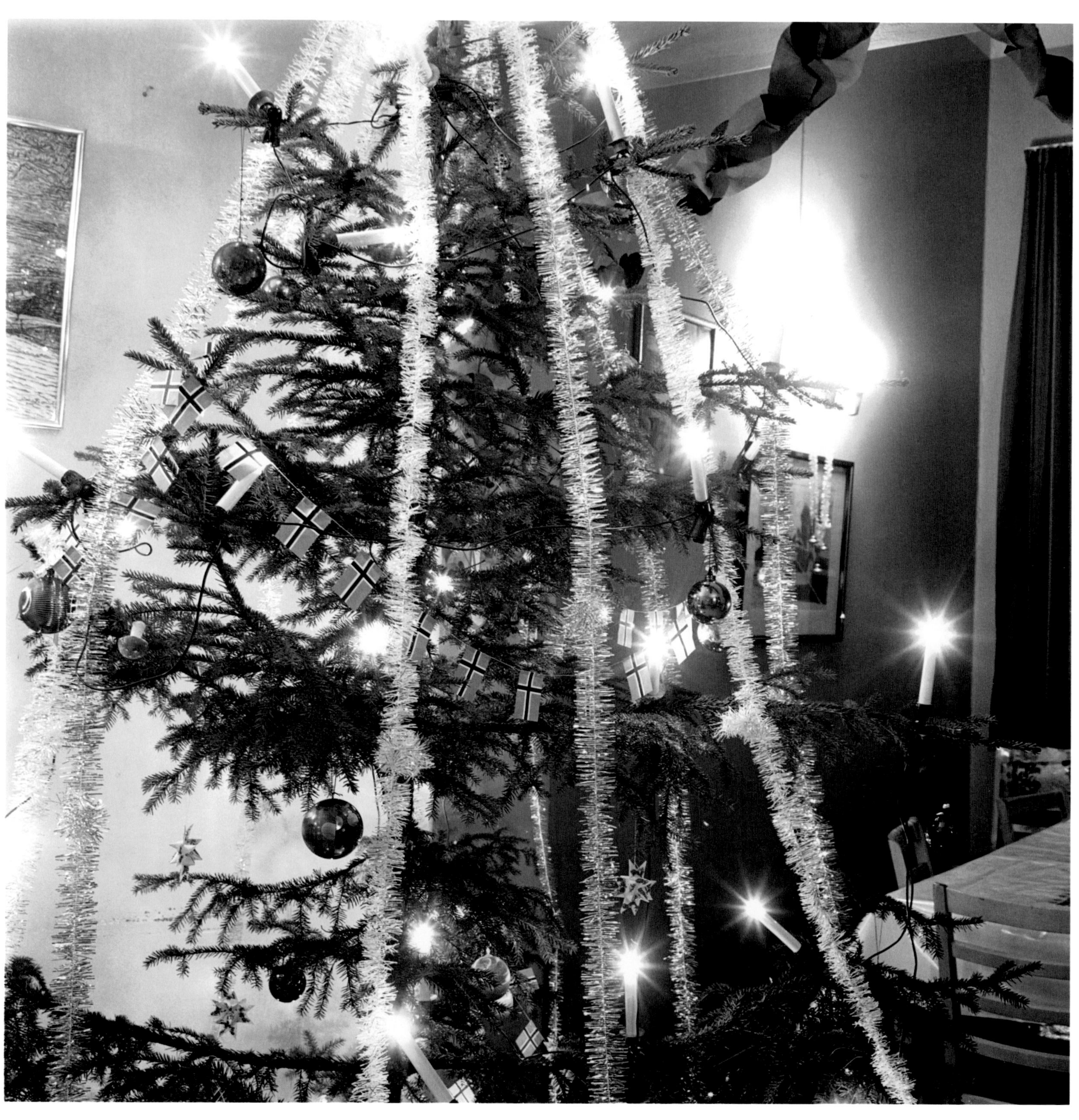

Christmas Tree. 1982

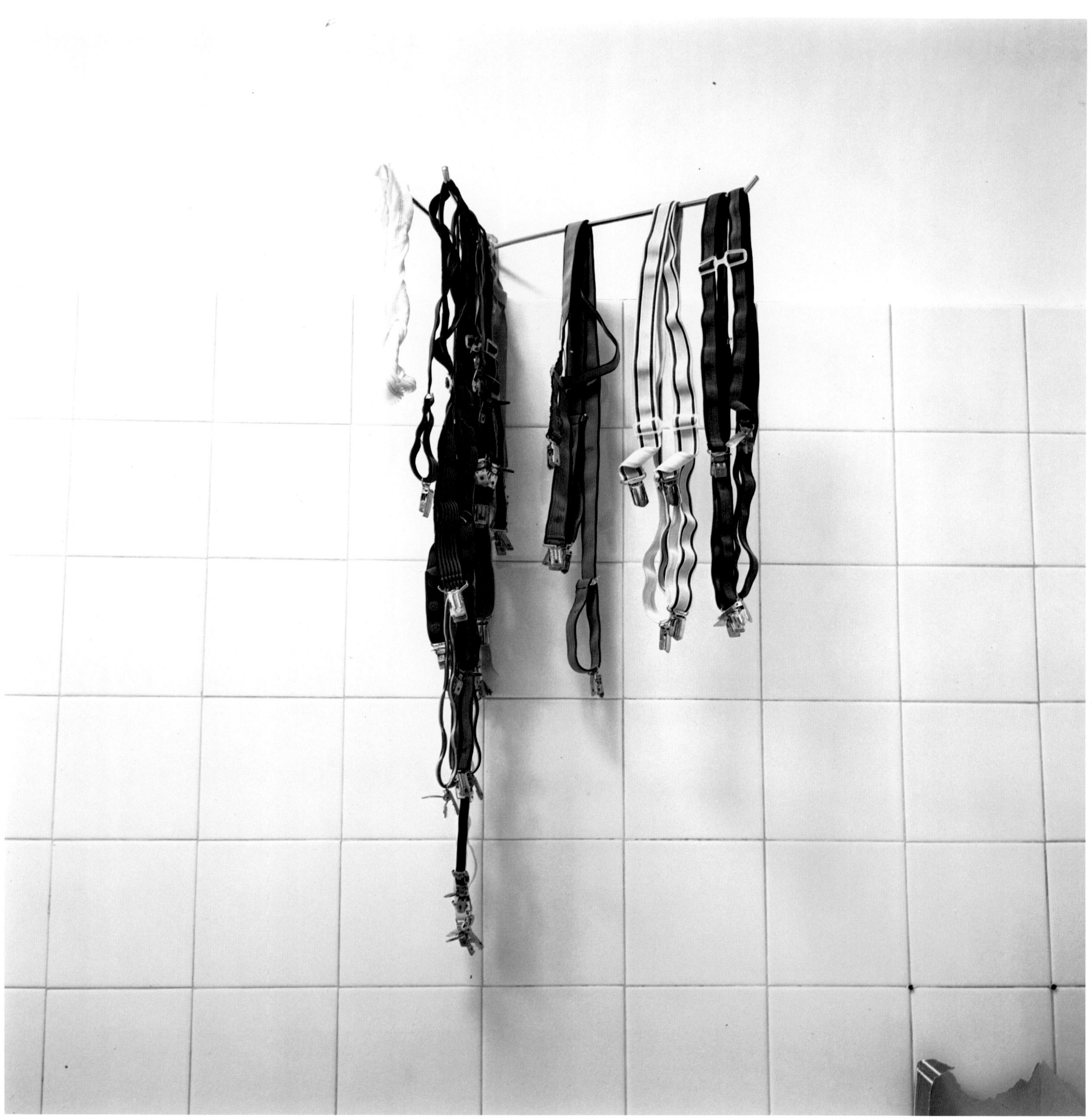

Suspenders. 1981

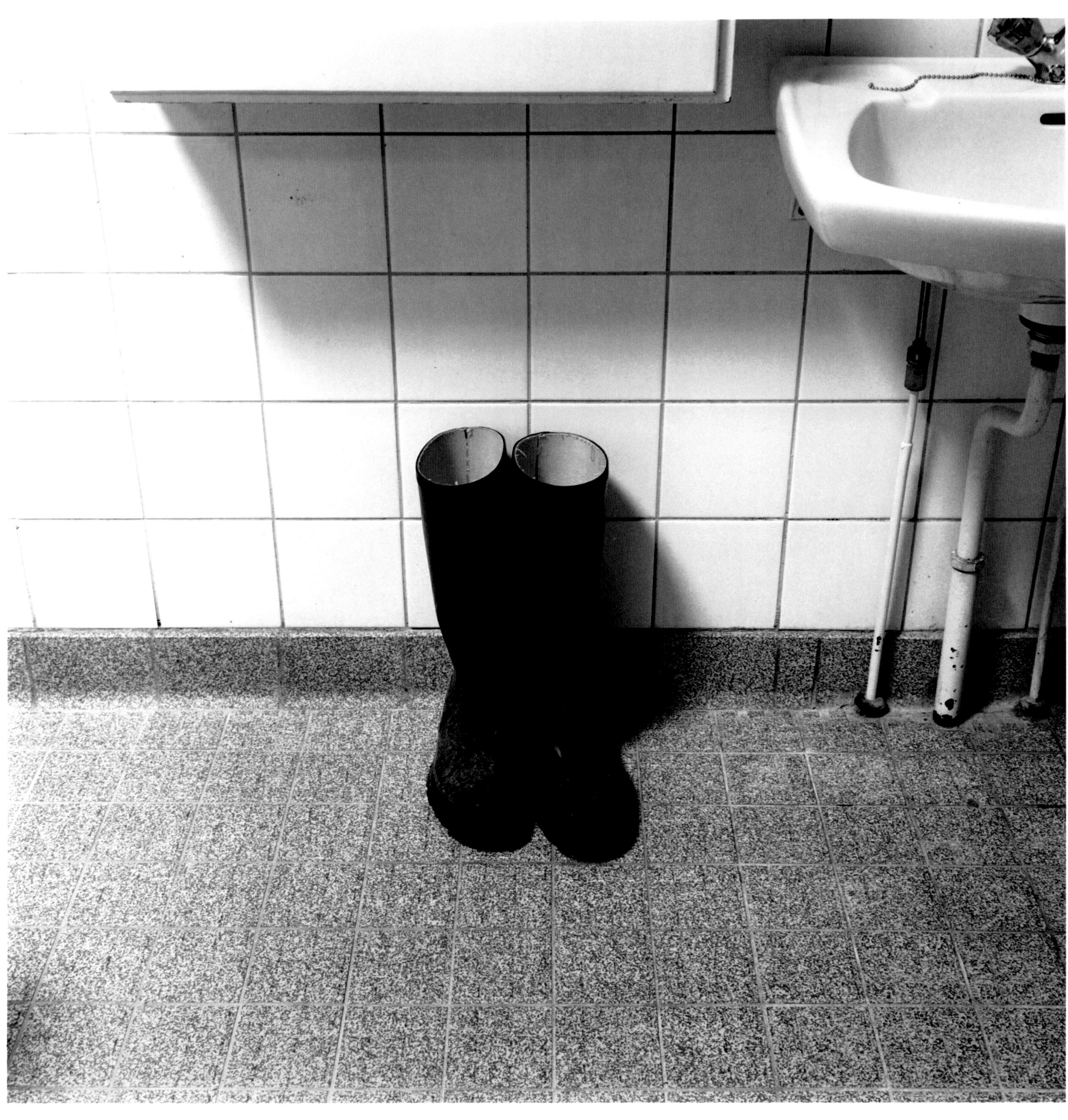

Wellingtons. 1982

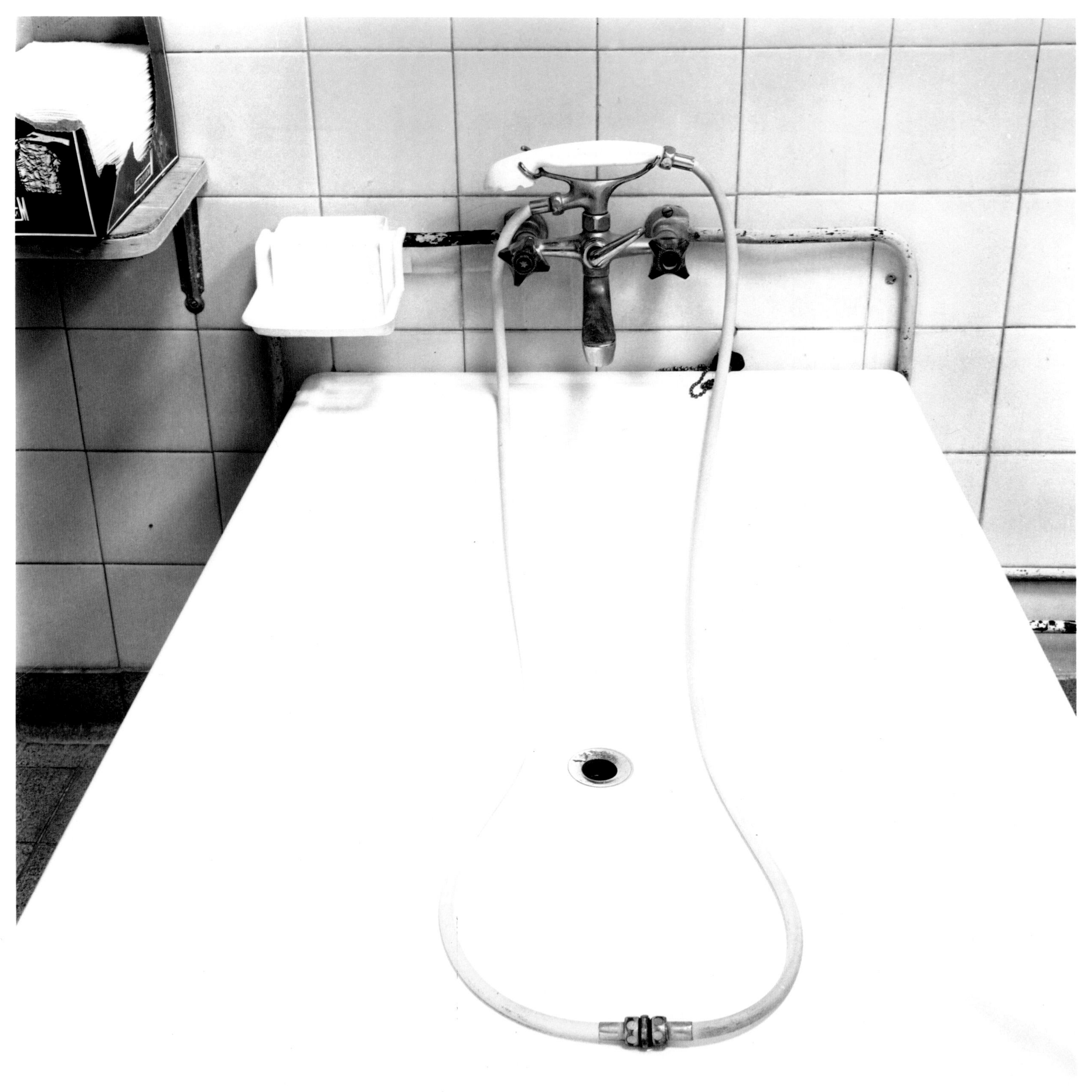

Bathtub. 1982

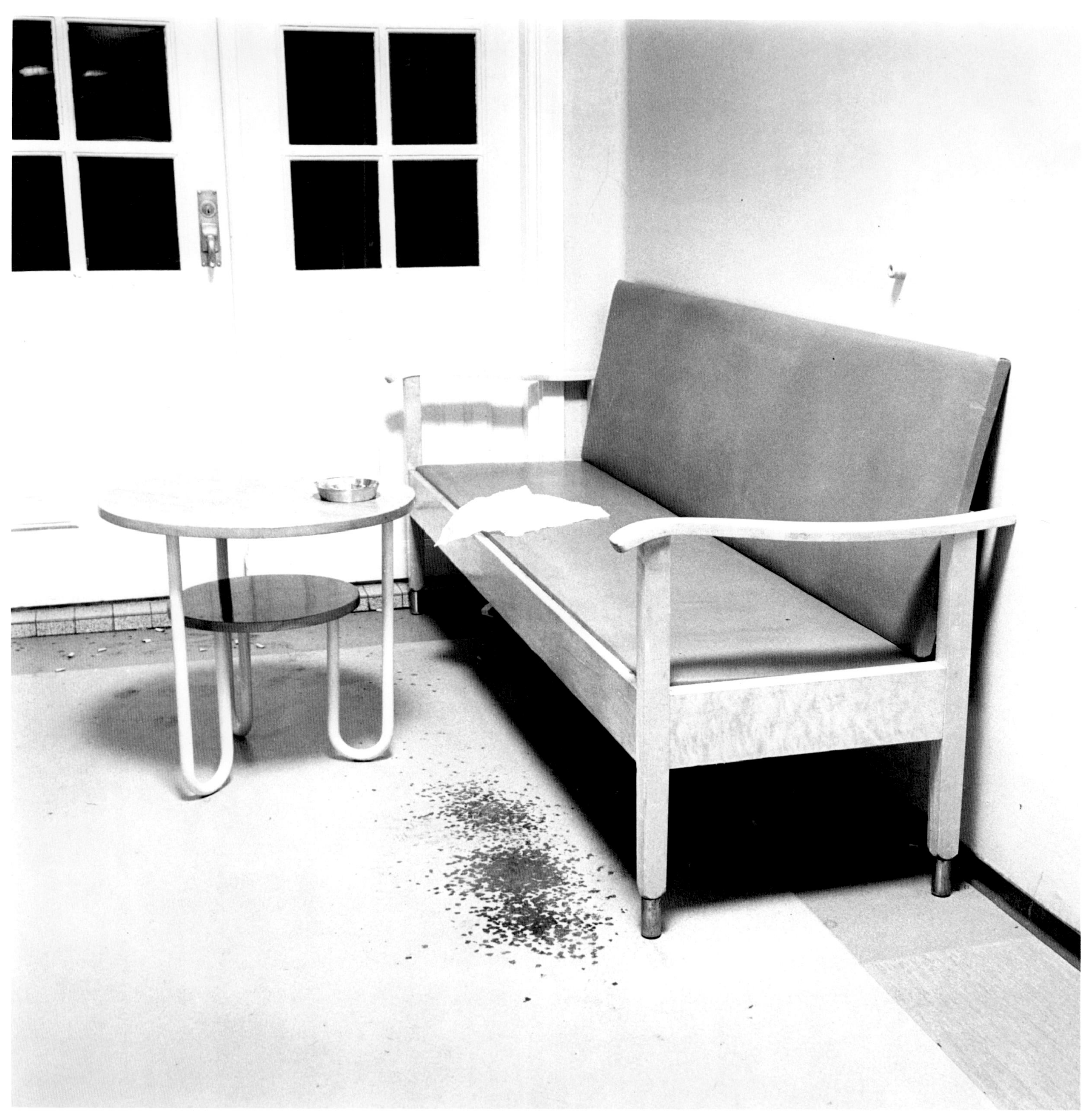

Floor with Cigarette-stains. 1981

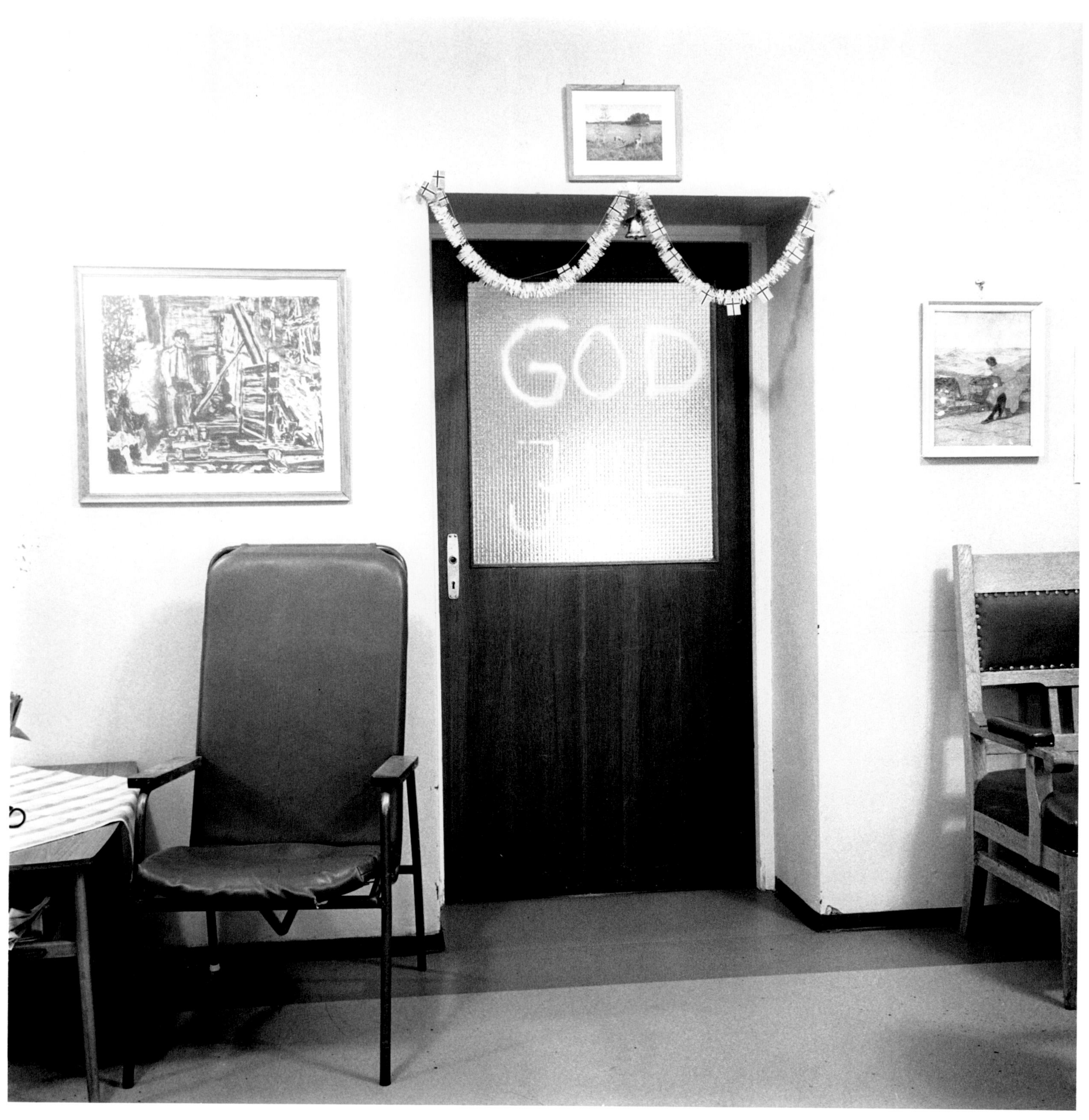

Merry Christmas. 1981

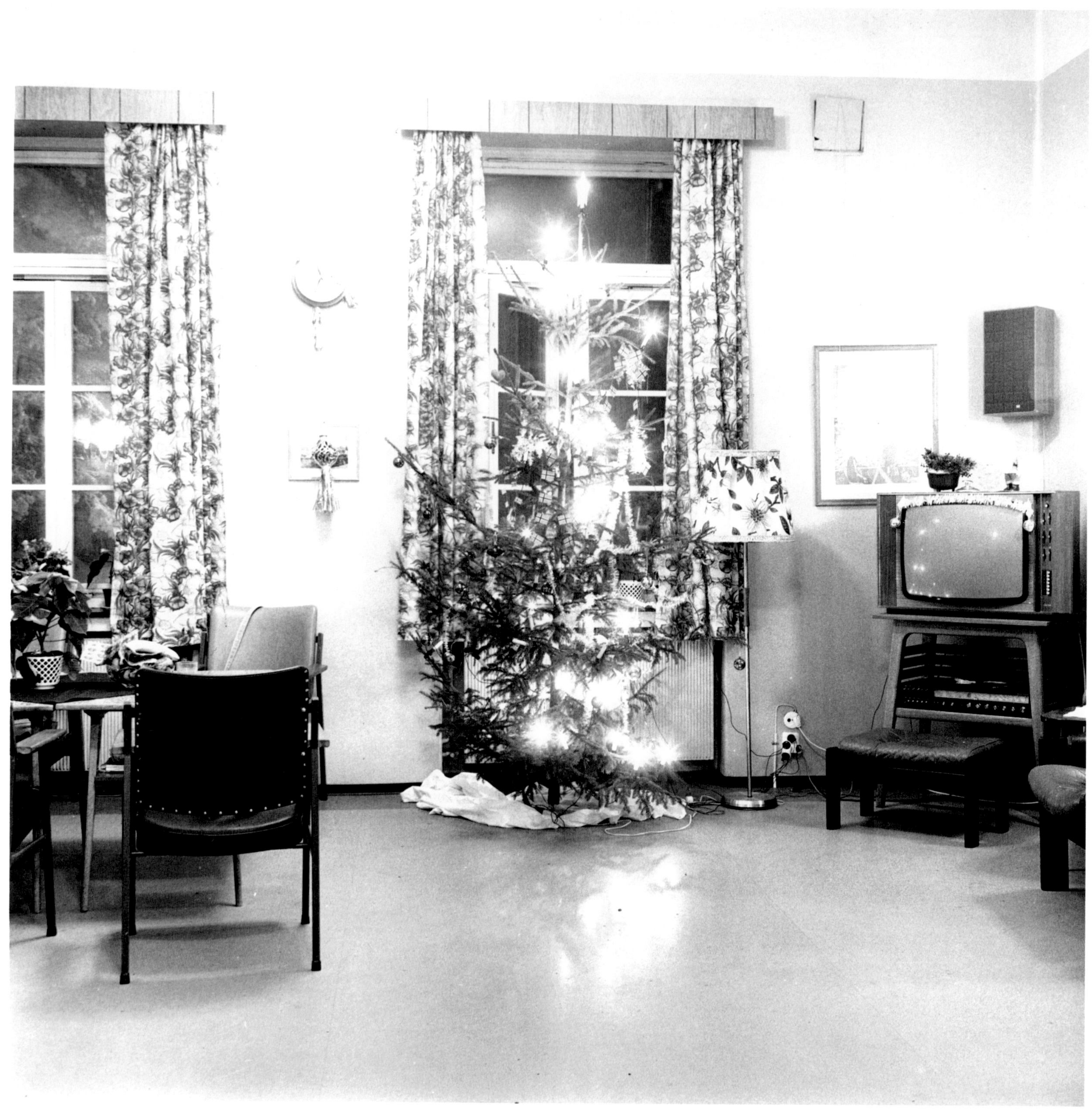

Christmas, Living Room. 1980

Dag Alveng: Exhibitions 1976-94

WALLS

Dag Alveng made his photographic debut with "Walls," an exhibition presented at the Photographers Gallery (Fotogalleriet) in Oslo, in January 1979. The exhibition included twenty photographs (23x32 cm), which were life-size reproductions of the walls of the room, each photograph a depiction of the section of the room it represents. The walls are white brick, and the photographs are subtle tones, ranging from white to grey.

EDGES

During the same year Alveng presented his exhibition "Edges," first shown at Galleri 1 in Bergen and later at Galleri 7 in Oslo. The exhibition consisted of twenty photographs, and was primarily comprised of pictures from the "54 Mayo Road." These were made in 1976-77, when Alveng studied in England. They were taken in his room, where he photographed the walls, door, bed, and a light switch. A text by Erling Kittelsen and the pictures were published in a pamphlet by the Ikaros Publishing House in 1978.

BLIND ALLEY

"Blind Alley," presented during the autumn of 1980, consisted of thirty-eight large (50x60cm) black and white photographs and an old radio. The exhibition was divided into three thematic groups: photographs made in pairs, photographs from France, and photographs taken one summer in Hvasser. The paired photographs, one of a log in the fireplace, and a second picture in which the log has been burned to ashes, investigates the themes of time and change.

Two other series were made in France and in Norway. The French landscapes show stone walls, gravel roads, and cows in an early spring, the moment before the foliage bursts into verdant leaf. Alveng's portrait of Norwegian summer, with its cherry trees, summer houses, and dazzling sunlight are empty of people, but traces of their existence and actions are felt in the pictures. The Norwegian summer pictures form a basis of the "Summer Light" series which was first exhibited in 1988.

THE POETIC THEATRE (DPT)

Relatively early on in his career, Alveng met a group of artists who were united by their mutual ideas. The group, "The Poetic Theatre," consisted of, among others, Viggo Andersen, Erling Rohde, Martin Roubik, Helge Røed, and Bente Stokke. In 1982 the group held a joint exhibition at Oslo's Kunstnernes Hus. Alveng's contribution to DPT was to photograph the process of mounting the group's exhibition, its first meeting, the creation of the art exhibited, and the opening of the show at Kunstnernes Hus. The photographs were later printed and installed in the streets of Oslo.

The DPT project was repeated on a smaller scale at Bergen's Art Association (Kunstforening). Alveng exhibited pictures from his "Summer Light" series as well as an installation consisting of a pair of large black and white prints (1.2x1.5m) installed on the floor. The photographs show a slope—in one picture covered with snow, in the second after the snow has melted. On each print Alveng placed sculpture of an eagle.

NIGHT/ MENTAL INSTITUTION/ ASYLUM

"Asylum" is an evolving project. Alveng started by taking pictures secretly while working as a security guard at a mental hospital during the 1970s. His exhibition, "Night/ Mental Institution," at Trondheim's Art Association (1982), included fifty photographs of the mental institution. The exhibition, which included the work of Joseph Beuys, consisted of a selection from a series of 107 pictures, a project Alveng supplemented with his book "Asylum," published in 1987.

In the series, Alveng photographs public rooms, corridors, and sanitation rooms. In contrast to other photographers, for example Mary Ellen Mark, who has documented psychiatric and social conditions at mental institutions, Alveng avoids photographing patients. In their place he photographs rooms and the objects in them, seemingly after everyone had gone to sleep. The objects in Alveng's pictures are witness to what might happen, and to what is not allowed to happen, in such an institution. An open drawer filled with knives, potato peelers, and other sharp objects, with a lock in the foreground, becomes symbolic of a potential danger.

The pictures were arranged in groups according to subject. One series shows walls and doors, another chairs and seats. Garbage bags, sanitation rooms, and corridors were organized in other groups. The exhibition was reduced to twenty-six pictures when it was shown at Kunstnernes Hus in Oslo (1986), Preus Fotomuseum in Horten, Norway (1987), and the Holly Solomon Gallery in New York (1993).

THE SHIPYARD AT SOLHEIMSVIKEN

This series was a joint project with Hanne Müller, master of social anthropology at the University of Bergen. The pictures are of Bergen Mekaniske Verksted (Bergen's Shipyard) in Solheimsviken, which was closed during the course of the project. Hanne Müller worked at the factory, newly trained as a welder, so she could understand the working environment from the inside. Alveng, however, never tried to become a part of the community; he merely photographed it.

The project, started in 1984, took approximately seven years to complete, and resulted in a book, which included text by Müller, and an exhibition at the Photographers Gallery (Fotogalleriet) in Oslo 1991.

A JOINT PROJECT WITH THE ARTIST SISSEL TOLAAS

The basis of this project is the moment of a horse's death, its decomposition, and the processes of change. Alveng began by photographing horses being slaughtered. Body parts of the horses were then left to slowly deteriorate. The decomposition was documented. Pictures of the horse's cranium were subjected to different chemical solutions, such as grease, paraffin, and oil. Parallel operations were carried out at sea, where fragments of buildings, boats, horse craniums, and skeletons were submerged in the water. How they settled on the seabed, and what happened to them under water, was registered with the aid of echo recorders and audio recordings. The project was presented at the exhibition "Photography as Art" at Sveaborg in Finland in 1985.

PHOTOGRAPHS 1976-1985

This exhibition at Wang Art Dealers in Oslo was an attempt to capture the essence of nine years' of photographic work. Alveng often works in series–independent projects where the series say more than the sum of the individual pictures. The exhibition presented Alveng's series in sequence, thereby creating an opportunity to grasp the fullness of his vision.

On the floor of a long hall, Alveng presented a conceptual project, which had earlier been shown at Trondheim's Art Association (Kunstforening), as part of Haugen and Maning's exhibition "KOKS." Pictures of snow-covered surfaces were immersed in water, thereupon dissolving. Time, change, and decomposition, constant themes in Alveng's work, were again investigated. The other section of the exhibition, on the first and second floors, were pictures from many projects, all of which were about qualities of introspection and meditation. These included pictures from Hvasser, the "54 Mayo Road" series, photographs from France, "Night/ Mental Institution," "Karl 0-2 år" (pictures of his son), and "Pictures of Men," a literary project undertaken with Trond Viggo Torgersen and Inge Matland. He also presented two projects about Norwegian industry, "BMV–Bergens Mekaniske Verksted" (Bergen's Shipyard) was part of a literary project about Solheimsviken shipyard and "USF–United Sardines Factory" about a sardine factory in Bergen.

SUMMER LIGHT

Alveng has been working on his summer pictures since the late 1970s. Numerous pictures from the series have been exhibited under the title "Frames, Hvasser" at the Preus Museum of Photography in 1982. The project was not, however, presented as an independent exhibition until 1988, at the Museum of Photographic Art in Odense (Denmark). It was also shown at the OPSIS Gallery in New York (1989) and the Portland School of Art in Portland, Oregon in 1994. In the series, Alveng photographs the ordinary, everyday life which we enjoy but never really notice. He is inspired largely by a garden surrounding a house in Norway.

NEW YORK

Alveng's latest project began in 1986, when he started commuting between Oslo and New York. In New York City Alveng photographs the city and the people he meets by chance on the streets. He calls the first series, consisting of single exposures,

"2 1/4." These pictures led to Alveng's later works, where he used a 4x5-inch format camera making double and multiple exposures. Because it is impossible to control the results of these compositions, and because coincidence plays a consider-able role in their creation, the pictures are unpredictable and constantly surprising works. Pictures from this series were exhibited at Galleri Riis in Oslo in 1993.

Andrzej Zych

Biography

1953-1974

Dag Alveng was born in Oslo in 1953. His grandfather was a printer and amateur draughtsman. His father practised photography in his spare time, and taught Alveng to take, develop, and print photographs. In his schooldays he earned money by taking class photographs. When he was eleven he saw the "Family of Man" exhibition, where W.Eugene Smith's "The Walk to Paradise Garden" made a particular impression on him.

He joined the Oslo Kamera Klubb and won a series of competitions. Some of the younger members of the club were involved with social reportage, especially as it was formulated by Christer Strömholm. In 1970 he visited Yugoslavia with his parents, where he made several pictures in reportage style. Some of them were printed in "Fotografi" magazine, but they failed to gain recognition in camera club competitions. He subsequently moved away from the camera club aesthetic and worked independently as a photographer. In 1972 he began studying medicine at the University of Oslo.

1974-1977

After two-and-a-half years of medical studies, Alveng took a leave of absence from the university. In parallel with his studies, he had continued to make photographs, and he had reached a point where a choice between medicine and photography was necessary.

Equipped with a selection of his photographs, he went to Paris to see the director of the Bibliothèque Nationale, Jean-Claude Lemagny. He also visited the editor of "Camera," Allan Porter, who advised Alveng to apply for the photography course at Trent Polytechnic in Nottingham, where Thomas J. Cooper and Paul Hill were teachers. Alveng subsequently visited Nottingham, which already had one Norwegian student, Tom Sandberg, and began his studies in the autumn of 1975. During this period Alveng studied the work of Minor White, Ralph Gibson, Robert Frank, Christopher Seiberling, and Ray K. Metzker. Metzker is one of the older generation of photographers with whom Alveng has consistently felt a close kinship. While he was a student at Nottingham he made the "54 Mayo Road" series, photographs of the flat where he lived. These pictures established a theme—traces of events—that was to be central to his later work.

1977-1988

In 1977 while he was still studying in Nottingham, Alveng and Tom Sandberg set up the Fotogalleriet in Oscarsgate Street in Oslo. This space was run as a private gallery and was one of the first galleries in the Nordic countries dedicated to photography.

Three years earlier a group of Norwegian photographers had set up a trade union, Forbundet Frie Fotografer (FFF). Together, the FFF and the Fotogalleriet were to play a major role in the development of art photography in Norway. The FFF pursued a rigid trade union policy, necessary at a stage when photographers had yet to win equal status with practitioners of other forms of artistic expression. It also promoted a traditional view of art, which held little interest for younger photographers.

It was the Fotogalleriet that was to be a gateway to a lively, liberal, professional ethos, providing access to cross-disciplinary activities, and foreign artists, introducing younger photographers to theory and debate and to a broad spectrum of other activities. In this way the Fotogalleriet fostered the beginning of a new Norwegian photography scene, and gradually received the broad backing of the majority of the FFF's members.

While he was running the gallery, Alveng also continued his artistic work, as well as his medical studies until 1978. In 1978 he produced his second series of pictures, "Vegger" ("Walls"), followed in 1979 by the "Sommerlys" ("Summer Light") series. He held several solo exhibitions and participated in joint exhibitions. In 1978 he and Robert Meyer launched a photography magazine, and he began to establish himself as a commercial photographer.

In 1980 "Asylum" appeared, and in that same year, he took part in the exhibition "Det Poetiske Teater" ("The Poetic Theatre"), together with other young artists who were working with conceptual issues. In the 1980s cooperation with other artists gradually became an increasingly important part of Alveng's activities, including projects with the artist Sissel Tolaas and the KOKS Group of Artists. During this decade he developed several major projects, often at the same time. He was in continuous contact with the art scene outside the Nordic countries, and he visited important exhibitions, such as "Documenta" and the Arles Festival. On the whole, the 1980s were marked by an effort to investigate methods of working in collaboration with other artists and the identification of new themes.

1986-1994

In 1986 Dag Alveng visited the first Houston Photography Festival, specifically to see the Robert Frank exhibition, and to arrange space for a Norwegian exhibition at the festival two years after. In 1988 he married Susan Kismaric, curator in the Photography Department of The Museum of Modern Art, and began to commute between Oslo and New York. He has continued to mount exhibitions, mostly outside of Norway. In 1993 the Holly Solomon Gallery in New York exhibited "Asylum."

In New York he has been working on a major project, which so far comprises 5,000 negatives of people on the streets. The pictures are double or multiple exposures and adopt a new, refined theme about time past and traces of events.

Alveng's pictures from these recent years can be seen as a step to investigate a new and immensely complex theme—the numerous aspects of humanity in the metropolis, especially distance and closeness, the horizontalness of the streets, and people's vulnerability versus the menacing vertical dominance of the buildings.

Per Hovdenakk

One Person Exhibitions

1979   "Walls," Fotogalleriet, Oslo.

"Edges," Galleri 1, Bergen (togehter with Roddy Bell).

"Edges," Galleri 7, Oslo.

1980   "Blind Alley," Sandvika Kino, Sandvika, Norway.

1981   "Blind Alley," Galleri-71, Tromsø, Norway.

"Blind Alley," Galleri KT, Kongsberg, Norway.

1982   "Frames, Hvasser," Preus Fotomuseum, Horten, Norway.

"Night/ Mental Institution," Trondheims Kunstforening, Trondheim, Norway.

1983   "Frames, Hvasser," Photofactory, Oslo.

1985   "Photographs 1976-1985," Wang Kunsthandel, Oslo.

1986   "Asylum," Kunstnernes Hus, Oslo.

1987   "Asylum," Preus Fotomuseum, Horten, Norway.

1988   "Summer Light," Museet for fotokunst, Brandts Klædefabrik, Odense, Denmark.

1989   "Summer Light," The OPSIS Gallery, New York.

1991   "The Shipyard at Solheimsviken," Fotogalleriet, Oslo.

1993   "New Works," Galleri Riis, Oslo.

"Asylum," Holly Solomon Gallery, New York.

1994   "Summer Light," Main College of Art Photo Gallery, Portland School of Art, Portland, Maine.

"Layers of Light," Henie-Onstad Kunstsenter, Bærum, Norway.

Selected Group Exhibitions

1976   "Photographic Spring Exhibition," Oslo Kunstforening, Oslo.

1978   "1001 Bild," Fotografiska Museet, Stockholm.

"Photographic Spring Exhibition," (traveling exhibition), Norway.

1979   "Norwegian Art in China," (traveling exhibition), China.

"Photography Here and Now," Henie-Onstad Kuntsenter, Bærum, Norway.

"State Autumn Exhibition," Kunstnernes Hus, Oslo.

"Modern Norwegian Photography I," Fotogalleriet, Oslo.

"Norwegian Photography," Satakunta Museum, Pori, Finland.

1980   "State Autumn Exhibition," Kunstnernes Hus, Oslo.

"Photographic Spring Exhibition," (traveling exhibition), Norway.

"FFF (Free Photographers Association, members exhibition)," Lithuania.

"Modern Norwegian Photography II," Fotogalleriet, Oslo.

1981   "Northern Lights," The Photographic Gallery, Cardiff, England.

"Scandinavian Photography," Centre Georges Pompidou, Paris.

DPT-3 (multi-media show), Kunstnernes Hus, Oslo.

DPT-4 (multi-media show), Bergen Kunstforening, Bergen, Norway.

"State Autumn Exhibition," Kunstnernes Hus, Oslo.

"Nine Norwegian Photographers," Camera Obscura, Stockholm.

1982   Biennale Internazionale della Fotografia, Caserta, Italy.

"Hvasser-series," Galleri Art-Aid, Oslo.

"20 Norwegian Photographers," Galleri Daguerre, Oslo.

1982 "The Frozen Image. Scandinavian Photography," (as a part of "Scandinavia Today") Walker Art Center, Minneapolis, Minnesota traveling to: International Center of Photography, New York; Fredrick S.Wright Gallery, University of California, Los Angeles; Portland Art Museum; The Museum of Contemporary Art, Chicago; Tacoma Art Museum, Tacoma, Washington; Kjarvalsstadir, Reykjavik, Island; Taidehalli, Helsinki; Fotografiska Museet in Moderna Museet, Stockholm; Henie-Onstad Kunstsenter, Høvikodden, Norway.

1983 "Session '83," Kunstnernes Hus, Oslo.
Young Photographer's Prize, Arles, France.
Pompidou Center, Paris.
"KOKS" (group project/one-person exhibition).

1985 "Art as Photography/Photography as Art," Sveaborg, Finland.

1986 "Nordic Art Photography," Museet for Fotokunst, Brandts Klædefabrik, Odense, Denmark
"Scandinavian Photography," Kunstmuseum, Düsseldorf.

1987 "Ten Norwegian Photographers," Houston Photo Festival, Houston,Texas.

1988 "Norwegian Photography," Houston Photo Festival, Houston, Texas. "Norwegian Prospects," Fotogalleriet, Oslo.

1989 "Z&Z," Wang Kunsthandel, Oslo.

1990 Photokina, Köln.

1993 "Positions 1," Fotogalleriet, Oslo.
"Summer Exhibition," Galleri Riis, Oslo.
"Summer Exhibition," Galleri Wang, Oslo.
"Recent Acquisitions,"
The Museum of Contemporary Art, Oslo.

1994 "Reports," part of The International Environment Law Conference, The City Hall Gallery, Oslo.

Selected Collections

Bibliothèque Nationale, Paris.

Fotografiska Museet, Stockholm.

Museum for Fotokunst, Odense, Denmark.

Stedelijk Museum, Amsterdam.

The Metropolitan Museum of Art, New York.

The Minneapolis Institute of Arts, Minnesota.

The Museum of Modern Art, New York.

The Walker Art Center, Minneapolis, Minnesota.

Bærum Municipality Art Collection, Sandvika, Norway.

Preus Fotomuseum, Horten, Norway.

Henie-Onstad Kunstsenter, Bærum, Norway.

Museet for samtidskunst, Oslo.

Norwegian Cultural Council, Oslo.

Olav Løkke Collection, Oslo.

Robert Meyer Collection, Oslo.

Trondheim Kunstforening, Trondheim, Norway.

As Curator

1989   "The Collection," Henie-Onstad Kunstsenter, Bærum, Norway.

1993   "Photographs From the Real World," Lillehammer and Bergen, Norway; Gothenburg, Sweden; Odense, Denmark.

Publications

1978   "54 Mayo Road," (with Erling Kittelsen), Ikaros Forlag, Oslo.

1985   "Pictures of Men," (with Trond-Viggo Torgersen and Inge Matland), Universitetsforlaget, Oslo.

1987   "Asylum," Koks Forlag, Oslo, in cooperation with Preus Fotomuseum, Horten, Norway.

1990   "The Shipyard at Solheimsviken," Alma Mater Forlag, Bergen, Norway.

Together with Other Photographers/Artists:

1979   "Norwegian Photography," Fotografisk Forlag, Råholt, Norway.

1989   "Z&Z," Fotogalleriet Foundation, Oslo.

1989   "The Great Outdoors," 1989 (appointment calendar), The Museum of Modern Art, New York.

Grants

1979   Norwegian State Establishment Grant.

1980   Norwegian State Travel Grant for Artists.

1983   Young Photographer's Prize, Arles, France.

1984   Norwegian State Guaranteed Income for Artists.

1994   Oslo City Grant for Artists.

Biographies: Writers

MICHAEL ALMEREYDA
New York. Born in 1960 in Overland Park, Kansas. Filmmaker.

PER HOVDENAKK
Bærum, Norway. Born in 1935 in Ørsta, Norway. Educated at the universities of Oslo, Berlin, and Paris in art history. Director, Henie-Onstad Kunstsenter, Bærum, Norway.

CAROLE KISMARIC
New York. Born in 1942 in Orange, New Jersey. Educated at Pennsylvania State University in psychology and philosophy. Co-owner Lookout with Marvin Heiferman.

SUSAN KISMARIC
New York. Born in 1946 in New Jersey. Educated at Pennsylvania State University in English literature. Curator at the Department of Photography, the Museum of Modern Art, New York.

PER CHARLES MOLKOM
Oslo. Born in 1946 in Bærum, Norway. Educated at Westerdal Oslo, Statens Kunstindustriskole, Oslo, Kingston College of Art, Kingston, England, Grafisk Høgskole, Copenhagen. Creative Director and Art Director, Bates International, Norway.

GERTRUD SANDQVIST
Moss, Norway. Born in 1955 in Uddevalla, Sweden. Educated at University of Lund in Art History (1983). Principal, Fotohögskolan, Göteborg, Sweden.

ATLE SKAGENG
Oslo. Born in 1956 in Oslo. Educated at the University of Oslo in Norwegian literature, history and sociology. Director and copywriter, Bates International, Norway.

ANDRZEJ ZYCH
Oslo. Born in 1965 in Zabkowice Slaskie, Poland. Educated at the Technical University of Warsaw and University of Oslo (Art History).

Without the generous support of certain individuals and companies,
this book would not have been possible.
Thanks to Per Charles Molkom, Atle Skageng,
Bates International, Norway,
Richard Benson and Thomas Palmer, Basberg Papir, Arild Holtlund and Torill Strøm,
Ex Libris Forlag, Øyvind Hagen, Merkur Trykk, Arild Pedersen,
Grønli-Gruppen, Knut Grønli, Gerh. Ludvigsen, Kjell Olaussen and Knut Østerhus,
Henie-Onstad Kunstsenter, Per Hovdenakk,
Michael Almereyda, Carole Kismaric, Susan Kismaric,
Gertrud Sandqvist, Jim Bengston, Per Maning, Per Schenk,
Michael Garner and Andrzej Zych.

Dag Alveng